MW01047800

www.deandrecarter.com

DEMAND GREATNESS
Success is Yours

"...a monumental shift in a new direction..."

DeAndre Carter

Demand Greatness
Success is Yours

Table of Contents 3

Acknowledgements 5

Foreword by Judith Haught, PhD 6

Prologue
THIS IS OUR MOMENT 8

Introduction
Lion Vs Gazelle: Success Is Yours 10

Phase I: POTENTIAL
Maximizing Your Ability 16

Chapter 1
My Dreams 19

Chapter 2
Who Am I 33

Chapter 3
How to Demand 53

Phase II: PERFORMANCE
Maximizing Your Action 67

Chapter 4
Running The Race: Knowing The Distance 70

Chapter 5
Coming in 2nd Place: I Tried My Best But… 83

Chapter 6
How To Win: Unleashing Peak Performance   **101**

Phase III: POSSIBILITIES   **114**
Maximizing Your Accomplishments

Chapter 7
My Opportunities   **116**

Chapter 8
My Advantage   **129**

Chapter 9
My Greatness   **138**

Conclusion: Join The Greatness Movement   **152**

About the Author   **153**

Acknowledgements

My Grandma for being the first person in my life to love and believe in me.

My Pops for always being a source of inspiration.

My Mama for being a strong woman while raising me and my brothers through the challenges of inner city Detroit. Thank you for sacrificing for us.

Jimmy and Kamal for always having my back no matter what the circumstance. Our bond will never be broken. Carter Boys 4 Life!

Quiana Rice for being my 'sister' and seeing my greatness at an early age.

Josh Gillespie for being my big brother and taking me under your wing when I arrived to Michigan State.

Rodney Patterson, your insights have shaped my journey in many ways.

Murray Edwards for providing support in some of my most dire times of need.

Dr. Lee June for providing a stable and stoic example of leadership in my life.

Aaron Decker, Vince and Val Green for your undeniable support, continuous encouragement and exemplary leadership in my life.

MSU students for allowing me to be a source of inspiration and coaching during your journey of graduation and success.

Andrew Devlin for coaching me through the darkest days of my life. Your enthusiasm, insights and wisdom changed me at a core level.

Savannah Grace Carter for being Daddy's perfect little girl. I love you so much with all my heart. Let's do this princess!

"The Avengers" (Jeffrey Brown, Bonita Smith, Janice Christian and Debby Ann Vickers) for your countless hours of support and prayer on this project as well as my personal and professional development.

Foreword

I am honored to know DeAndre Carter as a mentor and friend. DeAndre is recognized as a motivational force as he challenges people to **Demand Greatness** every step of their lives. He is ranked among the top speakers in the world by Toastmasters International. DeAndre also has a varied and acclaimed background as a businessman, mentor and academic advisor to students at Michigan State University, as well as in a variety of school districts across America. He has collaborated with the Lansing School District, Office of Cultural and Academic Transitions (OCAT) at Michigan State University, and Lansing Team Court to coordinate a variety of business and academic seminars for school districts and students of all ages. In addition, he has designed and facilitated empowerment workshops, including Leadership Development, Peer Pressure, Anger Management, Conflict Management, Values & Ethics, Substance Abuse Prevention, Victims of Crime, Bullying, and Shoplifting. He continues to motivate and challenge society to strive toward success.

His new book **Demand Greatness: Success is Yours** tells us that you and I are called together to create history. We have a mission that we must take seriously. Please read this book with an active eye, looking for key words, powerful stories, and life lessons to inspire you to nothing less than the best version of you. Regardless of your current level of achievement, there is ANOTHER LEVEL OF SUCCESS WAITING FOR YOU. Your ability to recognize the truth is essential to determine the likelihood of whether or not you will experience this new level of success.

Success is yours is a truth that connects you with success at a level so deep that no life event, outside opinion or inside doubt can detach you from the truth. SUCCESS IS ALREADY YOURS. You have the potential to seize the possibilities based on the level of potential you possess. Your performance is the access code to your unlimited potential. Your possibilities lead you to a time which allows you advance to the next level of unlimited potential you already possess. From this encouraging book you will learn what YOUR DREAM is, as well as to ask and answer the question "Who Am I?" You will learn that all greatness has a process. Knowing what to do is not enough. Commit to do what you know and you lay the foundation for growth and success beyond your greatest expectations. Every successful achiever has faced failure. Failure will push you forward toward winning. Winning forms character, grooms you for greater goals and equips you to win in all aspects of your life.

Open your eyes and see the greater opportunities, skills, talents, abilities and work ethics you have in your life. Learn how to put it altogether and *"DEMAND GREATNESS"* every day of your life.

JOIN THE GREATNESS MOVEMENT

Judith Haught, PhD
Founder, ARISE Learning Centers

Prologue

THIS IS OUR MOMENT

Over the years of writing this book, it has taken on many forms. I have many people to thank in the development of this life changing work. The first who comes to mind is Dr. Carl S. Taylor. He is an accomplished scholar and professor at Michigan State University; nationally recognized as an expert in youth culture in America. He saw something that would take me years to recognize. He saw that I would one day influence, impact and inspire people across the nation with my story.

We met during a movie screening on the campus of Michigan State University. I surprised many in the room by revealing that I came from a single parent home, my father was incarcerated and despite the odds I was excelling academically at a major university that had little in common with the environment in which I was from.

Dr. Taylor pulled me to the side after the discussion and created the moment; the moment which led to the decision in my life in which I choose to demand greatness. For every one kid like me there were at least 30 that were not. They were struggling in school, involved in destructive behavior, on their way to prison or in the process of doing so. Then he spoke the words that would continue to talk to me for many years to come. He said this, "They need to hear from you." I realized….

Then I had a story, now I have a message.

The difference is simple, but significant. At that point in my life all I had to offer was a story; a story of pain, struggle and ambition to overcome adversity. Now I am more equipped to provide a message of hope, inspiration, encouragement and empowerment. You will walk away from this book equipped to take your life to another level while achieving what you once may have only dreamed was possible. To not only be motivated for a moment, but inspired to create a monumental shift in a new direction that will lead you to experience life in a new dimension of greatness.

THIS IS OUR MOMENT, WE ARE CALLED.

You and I are both called together to create history. Just as I was called to write this book; you are called to read it. This is a mission that we must both take seriously. I have done my part. Years of sacrifice were poured into these pages. Now it is on you to do your part. You are called to read this book with an active eye, looking for key words, powerful stories and life lessons to inspire you to be nothing less than the absolute best version of yourself.

You my friend are called. Do not reject your calling. I have done my part, now you must do yours.

Together we must demand greatness.

Introduction

Lion vs Gazelle: Success is Yours

I looked her directly in the eyes and asked, "What happens if things do not turn out the way you want? What would you do if you had to return to your hometown?" "I can't....that's not an option." Why not, I responded. Her answer was eye opening, "There's nothing back home for me. I have to find a way to do better and stay here. I want to graduate from Michigan State. I want to finish what I started."

It was in that moment that I realized something significant about what she was saying. As an academic adviser I had heard many students share a similar feeling before. However, on that day something new occurred. I glanced at a picture of a lion posted in my office. It reminded me of the following story.

"Every morning in Africa, a gazelle wakes up, it knows it must outrun the fastest lion or it will be killed. Every morning in Africa, a lion wakes up. It knows it must run faster than the slowest gazelle, or it will starve. It does not matter whether you're the lion or a gazelle- when the sun comes up, you'd better be running."

The story itself was not new to me, but applying it differently was new. In the past I'd simply repeat the last line about running when the sun comes up. At one point I believed that it did not matter whether you are the lion or the gazelle. But in that moment I looked at her, and thought about many who came before her and realized the big difference between being the lion or the gazelle.

Both the lion and the gazelle are running full speed, giving it their all, but there is one huge difference between them....

The lion is running toward what it wants.
The gazelle is running away from what it does not want.

The difference seems small, but the impact on your life is larger than you can imagine. It means that the mentality you choose to take in life will determine how you live your life. If you choose the lion's mentality then you spend your time pursuing your dreams and desires; if you choose the gazelle's mentality then you spend your time running from your fears and concerns.

The gazelle mentality will allow you to be very motivated in short bursts of time to escape danger, but it does not inspire you to stay motivated to build a better future. It allow forces you to rely on external circumstances to bring out your best. You find yourself giving half effort until you think it has become urgent. You are not in control of your life, you simply wait for something to 'scare' you into action.

The lion is running toward its dreams.
The gazelle is running away from its fears.

Which type of life would YOU prefer to live?

The lion mentality inspires you to be motivated on your own terms. Those terms are decided by your dreams and goals. You set the tone of your life. You begin to believe in yourself more than ever before. Your life becomes driven by your hunger instead of your fear. As you realize that you have amazing potential to accomplish amazing things, you are on the cusp of something special. The greatness that has always been within you becomes more aware to you. This is the point in time where you understand that you do not have to wait for life to 'scare' you into greatness through the threat of negative circumstances. This is the moment where you can now look into the mirror, regardless of your life conditions, and demand greatness.

At the end of each chapter I will share tips on how you can develop the lion mentality in your life. My mission with this book is to help you to create a change, a shift, in your life where you will never be the same again. The change may seem small at first, but as you continue to walk in your new found confidence the results will be large. You already have everything it takes to live the life of your dreams. Simply put:

Success is Yours.

These three words resonate in my heart louder and louder each time I read them, see them or say them. They embody the spirit of this book which is designed to launch you into a new realm of reality. Regardless of your current level of achievement, there is another level of success waiting for you right now. Your ability to recognize this truth is essential in determining the likelihood of whether or not you will experience this new level of success.

Read the next three statements. Pause after each one and pay attention to your gut reaction.

Success can be yours.

Success will be yours.

Success is yours.

Did you feel differently reading each statement? Success can be yours allows your mind to imagine and wonder about the idea of success becoming yours. It states and focuses on the possibility that one day you could be successful. It is good because it makes you feel good about your potential. It garners and creates a sense of hope within your soul that uplifts you.

Success will be yours feels more definite. It has a more absolute quality to it. When you embrace this concept then success will not feel like a wandering idea. You will not be wondering, you will be more certain than ever before. It gives you a strong feeling. You will know that not only can you be successful; but one day in the future there is certainty that that you will be successful. The guess work has been removed. This thing is going to happen for you!

Success is yours takes everything to a whole new level. It is possessive. It is immediate. It is urgent. It is instant. This is the true realization that you are not only convinced that you can be successful or that one day it will happen for you; this is full assurance that you already have success within you. It is yours; in your possession right now. The key is to recognize it, nourish it and unleash the truth of it upon the world. It is your time to show the world what you already know.

Success is attached to you. It cannot be separated from you. The first two statements make it sound as if success is separate from you but can and perhaps will one day be connected to you at some later point in life. Success is yours is a truth that connects you with success at a level so deep that no life event, no outside opinion, or no inside doubt can detach you from the truth, success is already yours.

This new truth equips you to operate with a new level of power and belief....NOW! No more waiting on a better day or a brighter future to come as if you need an outside force to bring success to you. Success is yours reminds you that you have it now, it belongs to you and the idea has become one thousand times more real in your life.

There is not a choice of whether you will succeed or fail in life. You are already a success the question is: Will you walk in it?

You ARE the lion, not the gazelle.
You do not have to decide.
You were built to be the lion, are you going walk in it?
You were built to be a king/queen, are you going wear your crown?

Just like Simba in the movie, The Lion King; he was already a lion. He was already a king (in waiting). He didn't have to do anything to qualify; he was already pre-qualified. You are pre-qualified to be successful in life and live the dreams that you are supposed to have and you just need to simply walk in it. "Demand Greatness" will show you how 'Success is Yours'.

You are not separate from success. Success is already in you. Therefore, you do not have to pursue it success. You have to unleash success from within.

You may need to discover the elements of success within you because it's covered up, but just know that it is already in you!

I am here to proclaim and let you know that you are NOT a failure in life. The question is how do you unleash it? The answer is here. I have found an equation and chemistry necessary for you to become your best. Use this simple formula that has been given to me to share with you:

My Potential + My Performance = My Possibilities

You already have the potential. What level of performance are you going to mix with that potential to seize the possibilities that exist based on the level of potential that you possess in your life right now? Understand that the performance you provide will then go forward to 'seize the possibility' while also going backward to impact (upgrade or downgrade) the access level you have to your unlimited potential.

There's a temporary cap. Your potential is unlimited, but you do not have unlimited access at this exact moment. It's like being inside of a building with unlimited levels/floors, but needing an access code to enter the higher levels of the building. Therefore you potential does not change in life, but the level of access that you have at a given moment does change based on the performance you are providing in life. Your performance serves as the access code to the unlimited potential that you have been given in life. Your possibilities are experiences you encounter as a result of the performance you have provided.

A mediocre performance will grant you mediocre access to your potential and lead you to have subpar experiences with the possibilities that are available to you.

A peak performance in life will allow you to seize the possibilities that are available at that time. This allows you to then access that next level of unlimited potential that already exists within you. This is life unlimited, success unleashed!

You were built to be successful.

Success is yours.
You do not have to go looking and find it.
You must recognize that you already have it and display it.

Phase I: Potential
Maximizing Your Ability

Potential is where my success is present, but not visible.

This phase of demanding greatness starts within you. The most powerful principle about the idea of demanding greatness is realizing that it starts with your inner potential. Yes, it is your potential that is the starting point of realizing your greatness. It is at the core of who you are and who you can become.

I am excited about potential being the starting point because we all have potential. You are eligible to be great based purely on the fact that you have potential. This is life changing. Anytime that you do not believe that you were born to be great is a threat to your potential. Your relationship with your potential is a key to opening the doors of possibility in your life.

Maximizing your potential requires you to understand your potential. This simply means that you are aware of how much power exists within your potential. You are a unique gift, placed on the planet to do something in a way that no one else can duplicate. You are special. The amount of belief you have in your own potential will determine how much of your potential you decide to use in life. You are equipped with massive ability to achieve greatness.

We all have the potential to achieve amazing things, but life has taught me an interesting perspective on this topic. I believe that we have unlimited potential, but I do not believe that we have unlimited access to that potential.

When I would share this idea with my clients and students, they would always ask me to go into deeper detail. That led me to create this analogy that I want to share with you. It makes this concept more clear and easier to understand.

Imagine your potential as a skyscraper building that has so many levels that it reaches past the sky. You start out on the lower levels with an understanding that there are higher levels available to you.

Your performance is the access code needed to enter your next level.

Each level of potential automatically creates a possibility on that same level. That means that 'level one potential' creates a 'level one possibility' within your life. An example would be a student entering high school or college. As a freshman it is not possible to graduate during your first year. That possibility does not exist until the student has earned enough credits to achieve senior status. It is at that point, after earning senior status, where the student has gained access to the possibility of graduation. Therefore, as a freshman the student must perform to earn access to the next level, which is sophomore standing. As the student performs on each level they gain access to the new level which eventually leads them to graduation.

As we perform with excellence and grow in skill, we gain access to higher levels of our potential. In the eyes of others, it will appear that your potential is growing; in truth, your potential is not growing. Your potential has not changed, but your access to it has changed. You are growing into who you were born to be as you perform with excellence in your life.

Potential has a rare quality. Most things in life will decrease the more you use it. For example, when you have a pie, the more slices you eat, less of the pie exists for you to eat in the future. Your potential works in the exact opposite way. The more you use your potential, the more it grows because you are now accessing more of it than ever before. Potential is best used when presented with an opportunity because that allows for you to display your potential.

In chapters 1-3, I will discuss key factors that impact how we use our potential. You will learn how your dreams, your identity and your understanding of the growth process inspires your greatness. Paying specific attention to how you are currently using your potential will give you all the clues you need to start experiencing the success you deserve.

Chapter

1

My Dreams:
Where you want to be

"True desire in the heart for anything good is God's proof to you, sent beforehand to indicate, that it is yours already. That itch that you have to be whatever it is that you want to be, that itch, that desire for good is God's proof to you...claim it!"–Denzel Washington

Demanding Greatness starts with a dream that is alive within your heart. Some people in life are naturally dreamers. They spend time wondering about the possibilities in life. They push boundaries with their thoughts and actions. They live by the spirit of the quote from Senator Robert F Kennedy when he said, "There are those that look at things the way they are, and ask why? I dream of things that never were, and ask why not?" You may be one of these natural dreamers. For you, the idea of demanding greatness is ready made for your life. It is time to take action on those dreams in your heart.

If you feel like you are not one of these natural dreamers then I have news for you. There is a dreamer on the inside of you waiting to be awakened by your deepest desires. It is locked within your heart like a secret treasure. The key to unlocking that treasure can be found in the form of a question:

What do you want?

The answer to this question reveals your desire. One of the most important keys to living a great life is desire. If you are reading this book then I know one very important thing about you. There is a next level waiting for your arrival; you want more out of life than what you have right now, this is proof of your desire. We all have desires in our heart and mind that we have not accomplished yet. Clearly describing and knowing what your desires are will bring you one step closer to making them a reality in your life.

In my years of coaching and counseling people I have noticed a trend that stops people from success. Many people are spending too much time thinking about what they do not want and not nearly enough time focusing on what they do want.

When I hear people complaining about situations in life I will stop them in their tracks with this question: What do you want? Many times people are clueless to the answer. They have spent too much time worrying about what they do not want to happen or they have buried themselves in disappointment over what has happened. This robs them of the energy needed to focus on what they want. It also serves as a distraction that steals precious time away from them. This time and energy is needed to do everything that is required to make it happen.

The answer to this simple question can open massive doors in your life. The doors that I'm speaking about are not found in the world around you; they are found within you. The questions you ask yourself will help you to explore the world within.

Questions are powerful and when we use them properly they can guide us in the direction of our dreams. We must practice asking empowering questions that lead us to answers that will improve our lives. For example, the next time you are faced with a challenge think about the type of questions you ask yourself. If you find yourself asking negative questions then your brain will provide you with a negative answer. Have you ever said things like:

"Why can't I ever get ahead?"

"Why do bad things always happen to me?

"Why is my luck so bad?"

If you have asked yourself questions like these, more than likely your brain started to provide answers for each of them. This is because the mind works like a google search engine. It will provide what you ask of it, whether positive or negative. Think about this, if you typed 'do not show any red trucks' into google search, what will you see immediately after? Of course you are going to see a phone or computer screen full of red trucks. This is also how our minds work. Negative input is going to attract negative output.

The key is to be positive. One of the quickest ways is to ask positive questions. Here are a few example:

"How can I get ahead?"

"How can I make the best of bad things happening to me?"

"What am I grateful for in my life?"

Questions determine answers. Knowing this is important to living your dreams. It is necessary to start asking positive questions, especially about your dreams. By doing this, you are feeding the most powerful part of your being. This is the part of you that believes you can dream your way to a brighter future. This part of you believes in that quote by Kennedy when he said, "There are those that look at things the way they are, and ask why? I dream of things that never were, and ask why not?" It will help you to look at things that have not happened in your life yet and ask, Why not? You will start to look at the outside world with a new swagger.

As your confidence builds, the questions can transform into something even more powerful. They can transform into building blocks for confident action.

When it comes to achieving big things in your life, I have two simple questions for you: If not you, who? If not now, when?

Great dreamers master the art of asking the right questions.

Dreaming is the foundation for successful living. It is through our dreams that we truly live life to its fullest and have experiences that fill us with happiness. A good dream will rattle the foundation of your belief system and make you see more in life. It will make you look the mirror and see more than the reflection looking back at you. A good dream will make you see greatness within yourself.

Successful people have been dreaming throughout history.

Walt Disney was once fired from a newspaper because they said he did not have enough creativity. History tells us a different story. Despite feeling the sting of failure from being fired, Disney continued to dream. He did not let the opinion of others overshadow the belief the had in himself. One day he shared one of his biggest dreams with a friend. Pointing toward land what was mostly a swamp, he said this is going to become the happiest place on earth. Now, The Walt Disney World Resort is the most visited vacation resort in the world, with an attendance of over 52 million annually. Walt Disney believed in his dreams.

Oprah Winfrey was doubted early on in her career before making a name for herself on the national stage. She went on to create her own network and is currently one of the most powerful women on earth. Oprah Winfrey believed in her dreams.

Steve Jobs was fired from the company he started, before making a comeback that would revolutionize the world. He spearheaded technological advancements that helped to create new, innovative Apple products and restored the company to a position of industry leadership. Steve Jobs believed in his dreams.

President Barack Obama held a historic dream in his heart. Despite all 43 previous US presidents being white males, he believed that he too could become President of the United States. In his speech addressing the Democratic National Convention in 2004, Obama spoke about the hope of a skinny kid with a funny name who believes that America has a place for him, too. Hope in the face of difficulty. Hope in the face of uncertainty. The audacity of hope! This hope took on the form of a dream come true as he made history in 2008 by become the first African American to be voted president of the United States. Barack Obama believed in his dreams.

What are you big dreams? What do you want to do in life? Think about these questions and answers will begin to come to your mind. Spend time imagining your life as if your dreams were already true. This was among the best advice I ever received. In my youth, I would often dream about having a brighter future. I thought about becoming successful and leaving my struggles in the past. I was unsure about what I wanted to do exactly, but I knew I wanted to do something big. There were times I would dream about owning businesses and being wealthy. Other times, I would dream about being a two-sport athletic superstar. Sometimes I even dreamt of becoming President of the United States. The key for me was to keep dreaming. The dreams had to be big as well. The reason was simple. I was facing big problems in my life.

Dreams give you inspiration to overcome problems.

Growing up in poverty creates challenges on many levels. Usually impoverished communities do not have the best educational system. This was true for the Detroit Public School system. There were classrooms where ceiling tiles were caving in. Outdated computers kept us behind the technological learning curve. Behavioral challenges from students robbed the entire class of valuable learning time on a daily basis. Teachers were forced to divide their attention and energy. Their classroom management was a mix between fostering education and providing discipline. The challenges were systemic in nature and they were not limited to the educational system.

Crime is typically higher in poverty stricken communities. This was definitely true for my neighborhood. I remember times where there would be a rash of robberies. Kids would get robbed for their sneakers, designer winter coats or whatever the new hot fashion trend happened to be. Walking home from school became a concern at times. I would try to walk with friends as often as possible. This worked well in middle school years since my friends Bill and Edward lived in the same area as I did. However, they both attended different high schools than me which led to many more solitary walks home.

Typically if I was walking alone my awareness level was on 10. I would pay attention to people closely. I would know where they were, assess how dangerous they might be and have a response plan in my head in case anything jumped off. It was my version of 'keeping my head on a swivel', which is a term I learned watching football. Coaches used the term to remind players to be aware of everything going on around them.

Well, there were times where I did find myself having a mental lapse from this necessary way of thinking. One day it almost cost me big time. If you know me then you know I have a weakness for sweets. Donuts, honey buns, cupcakes, Twinkies and cookies were always attention grabbers for me. We had a local bakery made freshly baked donuts, pizza, bread and more on a daily basis.

I was so focused on getting a glazed donut from the bakery on the corner of Auburn and Joy Rd that I didn't notice that trouble had chosen me that day. Before I knew it there were 4 guys that I had never seen before. They were right in my face. The bakery was in front of me and of a set of bushes to my left. They had me surrounded in all other directions, I was cornered. They wasted no time going after what they wanted to know.

Him: "Yo! What set you claimin'?"

"Awww man….." was the first thought that popped into my mind. I cannot put into words the amount of unbridled fear rushed into my heart at that moment. I was in a position where I had no way to escape, facing a question that I know has gotten people hospitalized or even worse, killed. (And to think, all I wanted was a glazed donut!) Regardless, I knew that I could not afford to say the wrong thing to them. The problem was that I didn't know the right thing to say. I had never seen these dudes in the hood before so I had no clue who they were or what set *they* were claiming. So I did the best thing I could think of at the time….I stalled.

Me: "Huh?"
Him: "You heard me. I said what set you claimin'?"

Nearly shaking in my boots I realized that these dudes meant business. So I pulled on my inner Forrest Gump and played stupid.

Me: "Uhh, what's a set?"
Him: "A set, dude. You know what I'm talking about. Bloods or crips, who you claimin?"

For a second I was thinking that you can't define a word with the word. He should know that, but it didn't feel like the right time to say that. Now if I thought I was scared before, I was really scared now. Did he just say bloods or crips…oh God! I knew I had to think quickly on my feet; I had a 50/50 shot of guessing right, but then what if they knew I was lying. I felt like either answer meant big and immediate trouble. I was so scared that I stuck to the script, keep playing the dumb card DeAndre….

Me: "Uhh, what's a blood? And what's a crip?
Him: "What?"

Me: Silent look of utter stupidity
Him: "You know what. Forget this little dude man...." Then they walked away.

I wish I could tell you what he said after that, but I cannot for two reasons:

First, the huge sigh of relief that I had just dodged a situation that I wanted no part of. Secondly, I was so happy that I could finally get that glazed donut that I left the house for in the first place.

Looking back I keep thinking I was not there for all that. These dudes walking around giving people impromptu pop quizzes and stuff.

I made up my mind that I had to escape this environment. My big dreams helped me to stir up the courage and enthusiasm to overcome my big problems.

Remember this, as you dream big, do not overlook the power of small goals that can build up to your big dreams. I once read that a goal is simply a dream with a deadline. That means that you should dream big and then set small goals along the way to keep you on track to achieve your dreams.

This is one of the most powerful stories I have ever read about dreams. It reminded me that every dream will attract doubters. We must respond to those doubts in a way that will empower our dreams. This story is about a guy sharing how his friend overcame other people's doubts in the process of living his dream.

I have a friend named Monty Roberts who owns a horse ranch. He has let me use his house to put on fund-raising events to raise money for youth at risk programs.

The last time I was there he introduced me by saying, "I want to tell you why I let Jack use my horse. It all goes back to a story about a young man who was the son of an itinerant horse trainer who would go from stable to stable, race track to race track, farm to farm and ranch to ranch, training horses. As a result, the boy's high school career was continually interrupted. When he was a senior, he was asked to write a paper about what he wanted to be and do when he grew up.

"That night he wrote a seven-page paper describing his goal of someday owning a horse ranch. He wrote about his dream in great detail and he even drew a diagram of a 200-acre ranch, showing the location of all the buildings, the stables and the track. Then he drew a detailed floor plan for a 4,000-square-foot house that would sit on a 200-acre dream ranch.

"He put a great deal of his heart into the project and the next day he handed it in to his teacher. Two days later he received his paper back. On the front page was a large red F with a note that read, `See me after class.'

"The boy with the dream went to see the teacher after class and asked simple but profound question, `Why did I receive an F?'

"The teacher said, `This is an unrealistic dream for a young boy like you. You have no money. You come from an itinerant family. You have no resources. Owning a horse ranch requires a lot of money. You have to buy the land. You have to pay for the original breeding stock and later you'll have to pay large stud fees. There's no way you could ever do it.' Then the teacher added, `If you will rewrite this paper with a more realistic goal, I will reconsider your grade.'

"The boy went home and thought about it long and hard. He asked his father what he should do. His father said, `Look, son, you have to make up your own mind on this. However, I think it is a very important decision for you.' "Finally, after sitting with it for a week, the boy turned in the same paper, making no changes at all. He stated,

"You can keep the F and I'll keep my dream."

Monty then turned to the assembled group and said, "I tell you this story because you are sitting in my 4,000-square-foot house in the middle of my 200-acre horse ranch. I still have that school paper framed over the fireplace." He added, "The best part of the story is that two summers ago that same schoolteacher brought 30 kids to camp out on my ranch for a week." When the teacher was leaving, he said, "Look, Monty, I can tell you this now. When I was your teacher, I was something of a dream stealer. During those years I stole a lot of kids' dreams. Fortunately you had enough belief not to give up on yours."

"Don't let anyone steal your dreams. Follow your heart, no matter what."

–Author unknown

What a powerful story! There will be times where people are bold enough to tell you to your face that you will fail. You must be bold enough to keep the dream and give everything you have to achieve it. These moments of doubt from others are designed to tell our will. They challenge us to dig deeper, work harder and keep believing.

Below are some of my favorite quotes about dreams. I know that will inspire you just like they have inspired me!

"You should always dream one size too big because that gives your room to grow into them"

"Don't shrink your dreams to match your reality; instead upgrade your faith to match your destiny."

"It's impossible." said pride. "It's risky." said experience. "It's pointless." said reason. "Give it a try." whispered the heart.

DECIDE TO DREAM it will change your life forever!

Through the Eyes of the Lion

CHAPTER 1

DEVELOPING THE LION MENTATLITY

Through the eyes of the lion we can learn many lessons about demanding greatness. The first lesson is monumental: You are built to pursue your dreams. Like the lion you are destined to chase your dreams. It is natural for you to be in pursuit of the life you want to live. Unlike the gazelle, who is running from its fears, the lion is focused forward. You must learn to focus forward as well, when it comes to living your dreams. This idea is even clearer when you look at where the eyes of each animal are located on their head. The lion's eyes are on the front of its head. This allows the lion to have accurate depth perception and ability to judge distances when stalking or ambushing prey. The lion's eyes are perfectly positioned to look forward toward what it wants. The gazelle on the other hand is built differently. The gazelle's eyes are on the side of its head; built to be on the lookout for danger. You and I are built for success. However, sometimes we get sidetracked by adversity and challenges.

As I mentioned earlier, I began to notice these differences as I worked with students at Michigan State University as their academic adviser. MSU has a policy that places a student on academic probation when their GPA falls below a 2.0 which is equivalent to a 'C' average. When this happens, students are required to meet with an adviser to create an academic success plan for the next semester. As I worked with students who had experienced academic struggles I would ask many questions to gain a better understanding of the factors that had an impact on their academic performance. As you can imagine there were many factors: poor study habits, lack of time management skills, difficulty transitioning into a large institution and personal issues were among them. The answers that were eye opening to me came when I asked the question, "What would you do if you were not allowed to return to the university?" Student after student would talk about how it's not an option to fail. They would mention how they cannot go back to the environments that they had come from. Some were terrified about going back, but they were not equally as inspired to move forward. Most of them were not clear about where they were going. They had not invested much time thinking about what they wanted to happen in the future. However, they were sure of what they did not want to happen.

Where focus goes energy flows.

Constant focus creates constant magnetic energy. Living your life with the gazelle mentality means you are consistently creating the type of energy that is driven by fear. You become more in touch with your fears than you are with your dreams. In many cases, sadly, you can lose sight of your dreams. In the worst case, your mentality drops so low that avoiding your fears actually *becomes* your dream in life. This is where you hear people say things like:

"My dream is to not get kicked out of school"
"My dream is not to live a bum life"
"My dream is to pay my bills"
"My dream is to not have any problems in life"

This is not a fun place to live your life. You can only give your best when you are afraid of the consequences. When you are put in situations where there is no urgent threat, you tend to give a mediocre effort. Unfortunately, you have conditioned yourself to only give your best when it is the last possible option for survival. This type of life is dangerous for your dreams and ambition. It robs you of the ability to maximize your opportunities. It delays the arrival of your rewards in life.

The gazelle mentality comes with one guarantee:
You will never live your best life.

Be the Lion, not the Gazelle by learning to focus forward on your dreams and remembering that you were built for success

Chapter 1 Summary Activity
My Dream

❖ Identify three dreams that inspires you right now.

  1. _____

  2. _____

  3. _____

❖ Name one person who has inspired you to dream by living their own dreams.

_____

(*Contact that person tell them how they inspired you)

❖ List your DCMVP (Most Valuable Point/Principle) from this chapter.

_____

❖ Why did this DCMVP stand out to you?

_____

_____

❖ How will you use this DCMVP to change your life?

_____

_____

Chapter
2

Who Am I:
Who you are and where you are

"You can't be who you're going to be and who you used to be at the same time."
–T.D. Jakes

"Don't let your struggle become your identity"
-Anonymous

During the process of exploring your potential you will run directly into a question that must be answered with clarity. The answer to this question has all the power you need to move toward your greatness with unstoppable confidence. The question is, "Who Am I?" The answer to this question shapes your entire life. It forms your perspective. It influences your attitude. It also becomes the core that drives your actions.

An example of this can be found in the fable about the Scorpion and the Frog.

One day, a scorpion looked around at the mountain where he lived and decided that he wanted a change. So he set out on a journey through the forests and hills. He climbed over rocks and under vines and kept going until he reached a river.

The river was wide and swift. The scorpion stopped to evaluate the situation because he cannot swim. He could not see any way across this river. He looked upriver for a way across, he found nothing. The he checked downriver only to find the same result. Now he began to think that he might have to turn back and end his journey.

Suddenly, he saw a frog sitting nearby the banks of the river. He decided to ask the frog for help getting across to the other side.

"Helloooo Mr. Frog!" called the scorpion in an extra friendly tone, "Would you be so kind as to give me a ride on your back across the river?"

"I cannot and will not do that" responded the frog. "Why?", said the scorpion with a bit of desperation in his voice.

"Well now, Mr. Scorpion! I do not trust you. It is possible that if I decide to help you across this river, that you will kill me. One of your stingers would paralyze me right in the middle of the river." said the frog with concern in his voice.

"Think about it Mr Frog," the scorpion replied, "If I try to kill you while we are in the river, then I would die too. I cannot swim, that is why I need your help."

Now this seemed to make sense to the frog. But he asked. "What about when I get close to the bank? You could still try to kill me and get back to the shore!"

"This is true," agreed the scorpion, "But then I wouldn't be able to get to the other side of the river!"

"Alright then...how do I know you will not just wait until we get to the other side and THEN kill me?" said the frog.

"Ahh...," crooned the scorpion, "Because you see, once you've taken me to the other side of this river, I will be so grateful for your help, that it would hardly be fair to reward you with death, now would it?!"

Now the frog was a bit convince and agreed to take the scorpion across the river. The scorpion crawled onto the frog's back, his sharp claws prickling into the frog's soft hide, and the frog slid into the river. The muddy water swirled around them, but the frog stayed near the surface so the scorpion would not drown. He kicked strongly, his flippers paddling wildly against the current.

Halfway across the river, the frog suddenly felt a sharp sting in his back! Out of the corner of his eye, he saw the scorpion remove its stinger from his back. A deadening numbness began to creep into his limbs.

"You fool! Why would you do that." screamed the frog, "Now we both are going to die! What sense does that make?"

The scorpion shrugged and said, "It makes plenty of sense to me. I am scorpion and you are a frog. I stung you because that is what we do. Scorpions sting frogs."

This story helped me to understand why some people do things that set them back in life. They allow a negative identity to take root in their minds. This will then lead them to make decisions that have a negative impact on their lives. Too many people try to change the decisions and actions without realizing their rooted in a negative identity. Instead, we must learn to begin developing a positive identity. This can be done in many ways. You can read about successful and positive people. You can spend time thinking only about the positive characteristics that you possess. You can decide to spend more time with positive people who can point out the good in you. The important thing is to make sure you become committed to developing a positive self-identity. Our identity has a deep effect on everything we do.

Until you become comfortable with your identity it will be difficult to live the life of your dreams. The outside world is constantly trying to define who you are or who they think you should become. The challenge that must be answered directly is defining yourself for yourself. You must become sure of who you are in a world that is constantly pressuring your to conform. The surest way to succeed is to find out who you were born to be, become the best version of yourself and stay true to the real you.

Getting to know yourself will be a life long journey. As you grow, so will your identity. We all will change and mature over time. This is the process of becoming better versions of ourselves as we learn more and become exposed to new information. Many different factors and life experiences will impact how we grow over time. The 15 year old version of you will be different that the 35 year old version. Both of those versions will be ingredients to who you become by age 55. As you age, you will grow and change. Education will play a role in your growth. There will be a high school version of you, and possibly a college or PhD version depending on how far you travel along that path. If and when you become a parent, you will change. The point is that as life changes you must understand yourself at each level of that experience.

The mistake I want you to avoid in this process is searching for success before you have found yourself. If you find success before your find yourself, you will still be lost. This explains why some people have all the trimmings of life, but still feel dissatisfied with themselves. They might live in big houses, drive fancy cars and wear nice clothes, but they still are not happy. The void can be filled with a strong sense of identity and knowing who you are.

Understanding who you are is important because it will actually re-define what success is to you. Success is not the same for everybody. Some people measure success by how much money they have in their bank account. Other people measure success based on the quality of relationships they have in their lives. Career achievements are the definition of success for some people. There is an analogy that I like to share with my audiences to illustrate this point.

Let's say there are 100 people sitting in a room. None of them are related. None of them are roommates. They are all individuals who are independent of each other. Now let's also say that all 100 people have decided to go home once they leave this room. Once they left, would they all end up in the same place? The answer is no.

Can any one of them call another up on the phone and say, "You lied. You said you were going home but you didn't. I know because I'm home and I do not see you." This would not make sense would it? The other person would simply say, I am home. But my home is in a different place than your home.

The morale of the story is this, we can all seek to find a place called success but that does not mean we will all end up in the same place. Your success may be different from my success. Not only is this ok, it is preferred. We all have special assignments to complete here during our time on earth. Each assignment has great value which means you cannot get distracted by chasing another person's idea of success. You were born to be successful in the area of your purpose, gifts and talents.

You must also remember that the direction and actions steps you take are based on who you are and where you are in life. In order to reach the destination called success, you must first identify your location in life. Locating yourself means that you clearly define the next step that is needed on your journey based on your definition of success.

Think about it like this. If I were to call you right now and ask for directions to meet up, what is the first question you would ask me? Right, you would have to ask me, where are you? My answer to your question will then give you the information you need to guide me from where I am to where you want me to be. The same is true in life. If you want financial success for example, then you must define two things: your destination and your current location. Once those two things are identified, then you can map out how to get where you want to be. It works like a GPS. This technology is a great tool, but it requires some input to function as a problem solving device.

The path you take will be different depending on your starting point. Your journey may be farther than others, but always remember that you are not in competition with anyone else on the planet. Being the authentic version of yourself is the greatest reward you will ever have. The reward of being authentically you will help to attract all the other rewards you seek in life. The authentic version of yourself will attract the achievements, money, relationships, accolades, experiences and respect that you need. Do not chase these things. Become who you were born to be and these things will begin to chase you.

Nobody's opinion of you will matter more than your opinion of yourself

I remember reading a Norman Vincent Peale book ('The Power of Positive Thinking') where Peale was walking through the streets of Kowloon in Hong Kong and he came upon a tattoo studio. In the window were samples of tattoos available where you had an unlimited amount of choices. One of those choices was a tattoo that read "Born to Lose". He walked into the shop, in astonishment, and pointing to those words, asked the Chinese tattoo artist, "Does anyone really have that terrible phrase tattooed on his body?"

He replied, "Yes, sometimes."

Peale's response was still disbelief, "But I just cannot believe that anyone in his right mind would do that. The Chinese man simply tapped his forehead and in broken English said, "Before tattoo on body, tattoo on mind."

The moral of that story is powerful. Your perception of yourself will impact every decision in your life. The development of a strong mind is the key to a life of success or a life of failure.

The battle for my self-esteem has been long and fierce. I remember having a strong sense of self-esteem in my early childhood years. It was instilled in me by my grandmother. She always had the right words to say that put confidence in my heart and her warm smile gave me a sense of security. When I overheard her talking about me to other people it always included compliments about how I was such a good kid. She would always say, "Andre is the best kid I've ever raised" Every time I heard those words I would promise myself to never disappoint her.

She repeatedly told me that I was smart, intelligent, and handsome. She always said I would grow up to be successful. I remember how good it felt to hear her words. I did everything in my power to make sure I proved her right. I wanted to be the smartest kid in my class, I behaved well and avoided getting in trouble at school. I wanted my grandma to continue saying good things and be proud of me.

No matter what I said I wanted to do, my grandma would jump behind me with 100% support. When I played basketball on a crate in the backyard she would say, "Andre is gonna be the next Isiah Thomas". It made me feel like a million bucks! I enjoyed living with my grandma so much. Life seemed fun and easy, as it should for a child, but little did I know EVERYTHING was about to change.

When I was 8 years old, my grandmother was in a custody battle with my mother. My mother and grandmother did not get along well at all. As a child I did not know why, but it was a clear as day that there was tension between the two of them. I always felt awkward during times when both of them were in the same place.

There was a point during the trial where I was asked about my feelings toward each household. While I do not remember everything I will never forget being asked which household I wanted to live in. I was absolutely torn. I loved my grandmother with all my heart, but moving in with my mom would mean growing up with my 2 brothers Jimmy and Kamal. The thought of living with my brothers was exhilarating. In a moment that will never forget, I refused to pick sides. I told them that I liked living with my grandmother and enjoyed visiting my mom and brothers as well. The courts decided that it would be best for me to live with my mother and 2 younger brothers. The decision devastated my grandmother so much that she had suicidal thoughts. She told people close to her that she didn't know if she could make it through without me. Thankfully, they reminded her that if she did make it through she would be able to see me again. They reminded her that this was not the end. It was a new beginning. She had become so sad about the situation because she felt like I was going back into a bad place. She felt like there was no love for me in my mother's house. She feared that I was headed back to the same kind of treatment that landed me in the hospital in a coma as an infant.

This decision has colored the rest of my life. I had no idea that I was about to endure some very challenging times. The next 10 years of my life would be character defining years. My self-esteem was in danger and I didn't even know it.

When I grew up there was a popular phrase that adults told kids to say in response to other kids teasing about them: 'Sticks and stones may break my bones, but words will never hurt me.' Man I wish that statement was true, but they lied. Words do hurt and they nearly destroyed me!

Going from "slimetime" to primetime.

Growing up in the Detroit Public School system means that you were automatically a target for what we called capping. The generation before us called it playing the dozens. Today it is called roasting or trolling. Regardless of the names, the concept is the same, you crack jokes about people using whatever is at your disposal.

My middle school years were the beginning of my most memorable moments with self-esteem challenges. It started in my sixth grade homeroom class. We had a class full of characters and there was no shortage of jokes to go around. One friend of mine was extra light skinned. You could say his skin tone was high yellow. We gave him the nickname 'Sunshine' because we joked that the room got brighter every time he walked in. Another guy is our class got the nickname 'New York'. He was born and raised in Detroit so it had nothing to do with him being from NYC. Instead we called him New York because we had learned that the city had a reputation for being overcrowded. Every time he opened him mouth it looked like he had extra teeth squeezed into his mouth; it was like he had 34 or 36 teeth while the rest of us only had 32. So we called him New York because it looked like his mouth was overcrowded. One of my closest friends was guy who was a little chubbier than the rest of us. Randomly, one of us would run up to him and poke him in the stomach with our pointing finger while making the "hoo hoo" sound from the Pillsbury Doughboy commercial. Then there was my friend who wore glasses. We always called him a super hero because his glasses were so thick that we were convinced that he could see through the walls. We would look at him and say, "Hey man, you can probably see how many people in the hallway right now huh?" As you can see there was no shortage of jokes coming from this classroom.

Now you have to remember that in this class we were all friends so everybody was taking this in good humor. Well, there one exception that I won't mention because she got mad every time we teased her. Now of course the story also included me. I had a habit of constantly eating but never gaining weight. They would always wonder where the weight could be going because I was so skinny. On top of that I always had a big smile on my face all the time. This combination led to my nickname, Slimer from the Ghostbusters. While I felt I looked nothing like this green ghost, I had to admit that he was always smiling and food went right though him. Like I said, it was all fun and jokes in the sixth grade. However, little did I know that things were about to change for me next school year.

The seventh grade homeroom was a completely new experience for me. Nearly all of my friends from sixth grade were attending a different school or assigned to a different homeroom. There was only one girl from my sixth grade homeroom and I didn't even know her. My friends were gone, but the jokes were not. The jokes are all fun and games when everybody is your friend, but it feels much different when you do not know the people cracking the jokes.

My first problem started during winter. We lived 14 city blocks from my school which means I had quite a walk to school every day. In the winter as the temperature dropped, the need to use lotion increased. This affected me more than anyone in the house because I have the darkest skin tone compared to my mom and brothers. At home, we always had this extra-large bottle of cocoa butter that I would use before school. It was a huge bottle, almost the size of a half-gallon of milk. I'm only exaggerating by a little bit. The odd thing was that it only cost 99 cents. I always wondered how something so large could cost so little. Oh boy was I about to find out. Every morning I would put on the cocoa butter, but when 2nd hour gym class started I would be so ashy that my knees and elbows were gray. It was bad. My skin was so dry that you could play a game of tic tac toe on my leg. I know because I did this once with my brothers. Now I needed a plan every day at school for 2nd hour gym. I would try to avoid being embarrassed by rubbing water on my knees and elbows before going to hoop with my classmates. This always lasted just long enough for me to get back to the boys locker room and be ashy gray all over again.

My friends Jason and Lyndon would ask, "Dre, man how are you so ashy every day. Don't you put on lotion in the morning?" I'd reply, "Yeah, but it always wears off". They looked at each other and then Lyndon said, "Maybe it's a disease. You know how older people get Alzheimer's disease; well maybe you have ashtimers disease." The locker room burst into laughter. I wanted to laugh but I didn't think it was funny because they were talking about something out of my control. It wasn't my fault that the cocoa butter was more like an optical illusion than the answer to my dry skin.

I wished the jokes stopped there, but a guy named Kendell Taylor saw it as his mission to make sure they did not. Now, I gotta admit that Kendell is one of the funniest people I have ever met in my life. It was like he had a special gift and he was not shy about using it. He was an equal opportunity joke teller and so eventually I knew my time was coming. His first observation was my abundance of corduroy pants. I think my mama hit the corduroy lottery going into my seventh grade year. I could wear a different pair of corduroys for 2 weeks straight without wearing the same pair twice. We had all the colors too: black, white, gray, brown, blue, green, and burgundy. We even had sky blue! Yes, I wore sky blue corduroys to school. It's funny now, but I was not laughing then. Kendell figured that since I had so many pairs of corduroys, that he had to call me the corduroy pimp. Everyone in the class thought that was funny and they got a good laugh out of it every time he said it. I would tell myself that he was done and would move on to somebody else. I was wrong. What he had in store for me next, would become a classic.

Eventually the corduroy pimp joke became old and stale. So one day Kendell decided to change things up. He would say, "Man what's wrong with your clothes? Why do you always get things after they go out of style? To be honest, he was right about my wardrobe. I usually started wearing brands that were out of style two times over. One day he looked at me and said, "You know what, I'm not even gone call you DeAndre any more. From now on I'm calling you".... Wait for it...."DeBumBum!"

Everybody exploded in laughter! It was not just the words he said, but the way he said it. He said "De" in a normal voice tone, but placed heavy emphasis on the "Bum Bum" part. "de BUM BUM" rang in my ears day after day. It was a hit with students and teachers. That literally became my name at the school, I'm not kidding. It got so bad that even my teachers started using that as my name during class attendance.

By the 8th grade, attendance would sound like this: "Keisha, here. Joe, here. Bum Bum, here." Yup, by the next year, my nick name had a nick name. It was just Bum Bum and I answered every time.

While things were bad at school, in some ways there were worse in the hood. My friends compared me to every black skinny movie character and I hated it. When a movie called Menace II Society was released I got compared to the crack head who tried to trade some cheeseburgers (and something else too) for drugs. In sports, they said I looked like Manute Bol or Tyrone Hill. Then there was the time I was standing in the line at the gas station when I heard a little girl say, "Oooh, Daddy, Daddy, look...it's Pookie." If you have seen the movie New Jack City then you already know how I felt about what this little girl said. If you have not seen the movie then just know that Pookie was crack head played by Chris Rock. I couldn't escape his characters' most popular line, "It be callin me man."

Unfortunately, my high school experience started like middle school ended, with more jokes about DeAndre. Despite working at multiple barbershops as an adolescent, I faithfully grew a baby afro every few months before getting a low haircut. I became known as the Cody Chia Pet. At least two times a week, while the room was quite somebody would blurt out, "Ch-Ch-Ch-Chia". That was the jingle in the commercial for this product. One day a dude who rarely came to class made a cameo appearance. After one look at me, he took action. While the teacher was not looking, he stole a bunch of hall passes and wrote one to me that said: "Free hall pass to the barbershop. Do not pass go. Do not collect $200. Go straight to the barbershop." Again, everybody laughed because it was obvious that I badly need a haircut.

The icing on this ugly cake was the day I was walking down the street minding my own business when I heard this girl yell from across the street, "Hey! Hey you!" When I looked up I saw two girls. At this time I did not get much attention from the ladies. I was excited that this girl was calling for my attention. Maybe she was different than other girls. I had a glimmer of hope. Once she had my attention she said, "Hey, my girl thinks you're cute and she wants to get your number". Now I was both surprised and excited. This was my lucky day. There is a girl that wants MY number! This excitement only lasted a split second because it was interrupted when the other girl said, "Girl, don't make me beat you down for talkin bout I like that ugly dude!" Then 2nd girl shoved her friend in the chest and started to take out her earrings like she was really about to follow through on her threat. She only stopped when the first girl apologized and said she was just playing.

I was devastated. Wow, was all I could say to myself. My ugliness was out here breaking up friendships. This is starting to get out of control.

Saying that I had low self-esteem would be an understatement. I am telling you that my self-esteem was so bad that I would have been a gold medalist in the Low Self-Esteem Olympics. I had special moves and everything; I even perfected the "No Look Face Wash". I had been told so many times that I was ugly that eventually I began to believe it. I did not want to see my own reflection in the mirror when I washed my face. I told myself, "If it's that bad to everybody else, why in the world would I want to look at it". Every morning I would open the medicine cabinet above the bathroom sink so I would not be able to see myself in the mirror before turning the water on to wash my face. When I was done, I would say to myself "I hope I got everything off because I'm not about to look at this ugly face to start my day off on a bad note". This is no exaggeration. I did not want to see my own face.

One man.
One game changing statement.
My life was changed forever.

As you can imagine, after years of experiences where my insecurities were being used for amusement and jokes, my confidence was shot. These negative experiences started in the 6th grade and last until my 10th grade year when I had a life defining moment. Mr. Campbell was our African American history teacher. One day his lesson was focusing on all of the disparaging names that were used to describe black people in America during slavery, the Jim Crow era and even at the present time. There were very derogatory names being used to describe black people. Mr. Campbell's statement was intended to address the topic in a general sense, but I used it for my personal gain and applied it to my experiences. He emphasized how name calling did not signify truth. Just because black people were being called these names, did not mean that they had to respond to the negative names. It was during this lesson that he uttered the magic words that changed my life:

"You are not in trouble when people talk about you.
You are only in trouble if you believed what they say."

I promise you that day everything changed for me. I realized that while I did not have the power to stop people from talking, I did have the power to choose whether or not I was going to let their words have an impact on me. They could talk, but I did not have to believe what they said. I was so happy to know that I still had power in the situation. If you can relate to this I need you to know that the same is true for you. You still have the power and the final say in your situation. The words that other people say about you do not have to control your life.

That day in Mr. Campbell was the spark that I needed to become a better DeAndre Carter. I did not change overnight, but over time I did blossom in to a more confident person. Within one year I went from thinking I was a nobody to becoming the class vice president, joining the school TV and radio show, becoming the editor of the school newspaper, joining the National Honor Society, earning All-City track team honors in 4 events, winning senior class elections for most school spirit, best smile, most likely to succeed and Prom King!

There is a battle for your self-esteem and you will have to fight to win this battle. The key is to know that you are worth fighting for. You must be fully convinced of your value. We do not fight for things that we do not value. However, if something is valuable enough to us, we will fight til the death. If you knew how great you were then the idea of quitting would never stay in your mind. It might visit, but it would be quickly kicked out because you know how much value and greatness you possess.

You must fight for the right to define who you are and who you will be. Your self-esteem is within your control, but you may have to fight for it. Sometimes we are afraid to fight because we are afraid to lose. When the challenge seems overwhelming it is easy to feel discouraged. I am here to tell you that there are times where you must fight regardless of how you feel. You may feel like you are going to lose the fight, but you must fight anyway because there are times where you will lose the fight and still get the victory. I found this out for myself when a friend turned bully decided to put me to the test.

Growing up without my dad in my life meant I had to face every bully by myself. One time this guy who lived down the street decided he was going to bully me by not letting me walk down our street to complete my paper route. Initially it worked, I walked around the block to avoid him every day for weeks. I didn't tell anybody about it because I didn't want to seem like a punk, but the truth is that I was getting punked out by him. So one day I decided that enough was enough. I was tired of walking all the way around the block just to avoid this one dude. I braced myself and decided that win or lose I was going to fight that day. Surely enough he was there and ready to fight. It was the last thing I wanted to do because of his size and strength advantage, but my desire was bigger than my fear that day so we had to fight. Honestly he was surprised that I was standing up to him. It was a quick fight and I wish I could tell you that I put a beat down on him. But I didn't. I remember throwing a few punches, taking a few more and then it stopped suddenly. I later found out that it was his older brother that put him up to it just for the fun of it. Once I decided to put up a fight, it wasn't fun anymore so the 'game' was over. This story illustrates my point perfectly. Although I did not win the fight, I still got the victory. That guy never bullied me again and I never had to walk around the block to complete my paper route.

There are many lessons that I learned during those grueling years. The most important lesson was to respond correctly to my 'do or die' situations. The key is to DO YOU! When you have low self-esteem, you must find a way to know your worth, understand your value and embrace your gift. When you believe in your worth then you will have hope for a better future. This will lead you to the understanding that you have value. You matter because you are special in so many ways. As your worth and value increase, you will be in a better position to embrace your gift. You are talented and gifted at something! It is your job to find out what it is and commit yourself to embracing that gift.

Your dreams begin to become true the moment you start demanding a better you.

CHAPTER 2

DEVELOPING THE LION
MENTATLITY

The Lion mentality is at its best when you are fully aware and fully confident in who you are. For many years during my childhood, I was unaware of who I was. I did not understand the gifts that were placed inside of me. I was a difference maker, but I allowed other people's opinions to affect how I saw myself. The truth is that all along I had more potential to become successful than I realized. The difference in my life came when I began to see what was already there.

When I speak to audiences across the country I remind them that they are already the lion. Be the lion, not the gazelle is catchy so I continue to use that phrase to inspire people. However, the reality is that you are already the lion. Your true strength and ability will be unleashed once you realize who you really are.

It reminds me of a lesson from the classic Disney movie, The Lion King, where Simba had to learn an important lesson about who he was and what he was born to be. From the beginning, Simba was destined for success. He was the son of King Mufasa and when the time was right he would be groomed to step into his role as king of the pride. However, something happened his journey that almost derailed his success. He experienced tragedy, watching his father die and believing that it was his fault. His response was to run away from his troubles instead of facing the difficult challenge. It was at this point that he started to lose his identity. He met a few friends, a meek rat and warthog named Timon and Puumba. As Simba spent more time with them he drifted further and further away from his true identity. Instead of eating gazelles and zebras he began to eat bugs and grubs. Simba had turned into a vegetarian lion! It is possible to drift so far from who we were born to be that we start to act in ways that we were never meant to act.

The turning point for Simba came when he was reminded of who he was supposed to be. He saw a vision of his father and heard these words:

"You have forgotten who you are. Look inside yourself Simba, you are more than what you have become. You must take your place in the circle of life. You are my son and the one true king. Remember who you are"

Having the lion's mentality means that you find out who you are, what you were born to be and then take action toward your purpose in life. Knowing your true identity shapes the direction of your life. You must know and believe that you are great...right now! This belief will guide you to be confident in yourself and discover your purpose.

"The moment you start to embrace how you have been formed and fashioned is the moment you step into the very purpose for which you were created." –T.D. Jakes

Be the Lion, not the Gazelle by understanding who you are and what you were born to be. You will find power in your purpose.

Chapter 2 Summary Activity
Who Am I

❖ List three positive characteristics about yourself.

1._____

2. _____

3. _____

❖ In what ways can your positive characteristics create a positive impact in your life

1._____

2. _____

3. _____

❖ Name one flaw about yourself.

_____

❖ Can this flaw be changed? If so, what will you do to address it?

_____

_____

❖ What is your plan to address this flaw in your life?

_____

_____

❖ Name someone who saw more in you than you saw in yourself.

_____

(*Contact them to say "thank you for believing in me" and explain how their belief helped you)

❖ List your DCMVP (Most Valuable Point/Principle) from this chapter.

_____

_____

❖ Why did this DCMVP stand out to you?

_____

_____

❖ How will you use this DCMVP to change your life?

_____

_____

Chapter

3

How To Demand:
How to get where you want to be

"I don't like the idea of being selected. I wasn't selected. I demanded
my position"
-Will Smith

"Freedom is never voluntarily given by the oppressor; it must be
demanded by the oppressed" –Dr. Martin Luther King Jr.

Being a motivational speaker has allowed me to create many
memorable experiences by helping people to change their lives with
my words. I remember one time when I was speaking to a group of
college students who were entering their freshman year. Their
energy was through the roof and their ambitions were just as high.
They entered college as the best of the best from their high schools.
They felt like they had nothing but good times waiting for them

during college and beyond. They were ready to hear a dynamic speech and I was more than prepared to exceed their expectations. While preparing to blow them away I came up with the idea to enter the room with theme music. I figured that none of the other speakers at this event would have an introduction like that so I wanted to do something to set the tone that my speech would be much different than anything else they would hear. Now the question was, what song would set that tone. After some quick thinking the perfect song was playing loudly in my mind. I knew that I had to hit them with…the Eye of The Tiger! Let me tell you something, not only did it work but is set the room on fire. From the second the music started the room took on another level of excitement. It raised the expectations of my message in their minds. They were thinking, there is no way this guy can come out to Rocky theme music, get the room this hype and then fail to deliver. Of course, this was my plan. Raise the expectations, create pressure then deliver. I had used this strategy many times before in different ways. I knew how to demand an excellent performance from myself. I knew how to set a standard and rise up to exceed it.

This is important because during the question and answer session one guy made a statement that caught everyone's attention. "Mr. Carter, I agree with everything you said and you motivated me today to come to college with a motivated mindset to give my best and be the first man in my family to graduate from college" At this point, people are clapping and I'm smiling because those are the moments I live for as a speaker. Then he made another statement that shifted the energy in the room. "With all that being said, I prefer not to set goals or anything; that way I won't be disappointed." It was at that moment that I realized what was happening within him. He was dealing with a familiar challenge; the one where we want a better life but fear the possibility of falling short of our goals and expectations. Very few things in life hurt more than unfulfilled expectations.

The entire room received a very valuable life lesson that day. My response was simple. You cannot avoid disappointment in life, but you can determine what role it will play in your life. I explained that we have all been disappointed by someone or something in our lives. It was not the first time nor the last time. The key is to make sure the disappointment occurs in a way that is teaching you lessons as you strive to create a better future for yourself and the world around you. After the speech, he came up to shake my hand and say thank you. He admitted that his fears were influencing how he approached his goals. Then he committed himself to focusing more finding ways to succeed instead of looking for ways not to fail. In sports this is called playing to win versus playing not to lose. The team who decides to play the game in a way that focuses on winning usually beats out the team who is simply trying not to lose. Set your sights high and refuse to lower them because of fear.

It is true that you will face risks by setting expectations for yourself in life; but expectations are required for you to live your dreams. The greatest risk in life is deciding not to take any risks at all. The process of demanding greatness requires you to elevate the expectations you have placed on yourself and then upgrade your actions to meet and exceed those expectations. So like I shared with that young man years ago, I'm sharing the same message with you. The disappointment you might face from chasing your dreams may hurt along the way, but it will not hurt nearly as much as the disappointment you feel when you never challenge yourself to give your best. You become your best by creating expectations and setting goals to strive for.

Hopes deferred makes the heart sick; do not become a sick hearted unfulfilled talent.

All greatness has a process. This process begins with an understanding of how to make the process work for you. Once you have an understanding of how to demand greatness from yourself, then you are equipped to demand greatness from life while teaching others to do the same. A demand is simply a requirement that you have placed on a person or situation. Demanding greatness is a way of saying that you are requiring greatness from yourself. That is the standard that you will use to guide your through life.

If you want a great example of how to place a demand then look no further than a child who has their sights set on something they want. Any parent will tell you that the best salesperson on the planet is a child obsessed with something they want. Children become extremely persistent, creative and aware when they are in this mode. Whether you realize it or not they are paying attention to all the signs. They are laser focused on the object of their affection and they do not give up until they have it. They will use your own words against you, "Well, you said…" They will time their request by waiting until you're occupied or distracted by something to slide their question under your radar. They will do whatever it takes. We can learn a lot from how committed a child can be toward their goal.

I had to demand greatness from myself on many occasions. Today I am an award winning speaker, published author and first generation graduate from a major four year institution. That journey included many moments where I had to face my doubts head on. My high school's average GPA was a 1.6 and average ACT score was 14. These numbers were not ideal and could not even be close to considered 'college prep'. In short, I was not academically prepared to attend Michigan State University based on my high school experience. I did not allow this lack of preparation to intimidate me. I adopted an attitude that said I will do whatever it takes to achieve my dream of graduating from college. Thankfully I believe that where are you going is more important that where you are from.

Action is the best way to face your fears.
Flawless Pebble vs Flawed Diamond

In the words of the great Chinese philosopher Confucius, "Better a diamond with a flaw than a pebble without." We must be willing to acknowledge our flaws as we pursue our dreams. Fear has stopped too many people on the road to greatness. Too often we are afraid of what people will say about us if we fail. We worry about being perceived as not good enough.

I was watching a TV show where an extremely talented recording artist was asked by one of her fans, "You have one of the most beautiful voices I have ever heard. I just love it. When are you going to record a solo album?" Her response to the question was jarring. You could see the fear on her face as she explained how she was afraid to fail on a solo project. She was a member of a music group, which had successfully recorded hit songs and was even signed as a solo artist after her time with the group was over. The only thing left for her to do was to accept her status as a flawed diamond. However, because she was full of fear instead of being fueled by faith, her entire future was frozen based on the fears from her past.

The dangerous thing about a situation like that is the effects it has on your mentality. Fear of failure can lead to a self-fulfilling prophecy where you create situations of failure to validate your belief that you do not have what it takes to be successful. When talented people do this to themselves they create what I call success atrophy. They start rationalizing why they are not farther along in life. They begin to sell themselves on a story that says "I'm ok with where I am", knowing in their heart that they really want more out of life. They come up with a list of excuses to explain why they are not trying as hard as they can to live their dreams. Some even go as far as doing a "dream transfer" and try to live their dreams through their kids or other people in their lives.

The word atrophy has its roots in the field of medicine. It is most commonly used to describe a partial or completed wasting aware of a part of the body. That's what happens to us if we are not facing challenges and pursuing our dreams, we allow our talents to waste away. The longer you allow this to happen, the more difficult it becomes to reach your full potential. If you were strapped to a chair for weeks and then tried to get up and walk you would most likely fall flat on your face. Atrophy is the reason, the less you use your body the more it begins to waste away. This is why some people pass away shortly after retiring if they do not take up hobbies and activities that keep them active. You can avoid falling victim to success atrophy by finding ways to use your talents consistently. During a time where I was feeling like this, I joined a group called Toastmasters International. Toastmasters International is an organization focused on developing leaders and improving skills as a speaker. Les Brown taught me that it is important to involve yourself in at least one thing that validates you as a person of value. I knew that joining Toastmasters would help me to feel good about my ability to speak and motivate others. It worked!

You and I can learn a lesson from the fearful recording artist. Be the best you can be today knowing that tomorrow your best can become a little bit better. We cannot be afraid to step out of the limb from time to time; besides the fruit is always found on the limb of the tree anyway. Diamonds do not have to be perfect to have value. We cannot afford to spend our lives trying to be a perfect pebble when your dreams are connected to your willingness to be a damaged diamond. Remember that the damage does not last forever. You can improve, get better and reduce your weaknesses. But you first must be willing to expose them in the process of chasing greatness.

The will to succeed is sustained by the will to prepare. Many people believe that success is about luck, but fail to understand that chance and 'luck' favors the prepared man or woman. Luck is when preparation meets opportunity. You will be presented one day with the opportunity of a lifetime, the question is "Will you be ready?"

Live your life with a sense of purpose.
Life is going reward you as soon as it sees (the real) you.

Life is waiting on you to do what you were born to do. You were built for success; you were made to be great. You are supposed to be phenomenal.

As soon as life sees you doing what you are supposed to do, committing and giving effort, as soon as you focus and lock in on the goal of fulfilling your purpose THEN your life will change for the better, forever!

You might be thinking, "But DeAndre, life has not been rewarding me. Life has not been complimenting me. Things have not happened the way you are explaining it to me. I have success, I have accomplishments, but I do not have peace."

Life will do it, as soon as you show yourself. Many people have told me, "but I've been here". I have to remind them that what they are saying is not true, YOU haven't been here. Instead you have sent your representative. You have sent an imposter version of yourself.

The imposter version has doubts. It is that lesser version of you that does not believe in your greatness and potential. This weaker version of you will constantly desire to conform and lower the standards of expectation. You cannot allow this version of yourself to control your life.

When I first started speaking it was obvious who I was learning from. My first introduction to motivational speaking was through a Les Brown cassette tape titled, "It's Hard". It was from a six part message he delivered where he inspired his audience to choose their future and live their dreams. I could not stop listening to the powerful words he was sharing. I told myself, I wish I could do that.

The next speaker I learned from was Zig Ziglar. He was a motivating speaker with a very unique delivery style. His accent quickly became as stuck in my head as his inspirational stories. Zig did a phenomenal job of painting word pictures in my mind where I could see myself becoming more successful that I had ever dreamed.

The point I'm making is simple. If Les Brown and Zig Ziglar made a baby, it would be named DeAndre Carter. That is how much I learned from their speaking styles and life experiences. My first few years were nearly carbon copies of their messages. I experienced some progress as a speaker, but I was not experiencing the success I deserved. Why? Because I had not shown up yet. The real DeAndre Carter was not on the scene. It was not until I grew into my own personal style of speaking that I started to see what was destined for me all along.

It is common to admire people and decide to learn from them. I do not see anything wrong with starting out new challenges by learning lessons from successful people. The key is to make sure you grow from that starting point to develop your own uniqueness.

When the real you shows up then you begin to see, think, talk and act like the unique person that only YOU can be.

Fire the imposter and hire yourself for greatness.

The imposter will say that the real you does not have talent to succeed. It will say that you are not destined for success. That is lie; you are built to be successful. It is in your DNA, you couldn't get rid of it if you wanted to. All you can do is hide it through inaction and indecision.

Remember that you playing small does not serve the world. Get out here and do what you're supposed to do. Show us the greatness that has been put inside of you.

Make your presence felt.

There is a new level of pure confidence that you have yet to tap into because you are not walking in purpose. Purpose will perfectly equip you with the right amount of confidence and humility at the same time. You will be sure of yourself in ways that you may never have experienced before. You will believe in every move that you do and have faith in every project you undertake. However, you will be humbled by the understanding that your purpose was not self-assigned. True purpose is given. My personal belief is that it comes from God. You are not obligated to share that belief; but I am obligated to broadcast that mine originates from Him. This perfect mix of confidence and humility will allow you to put others in awe and put yourself in position to experience true success.

True success is significance.

Significance is the ability to walk in your purpose, inspire and serve others to enhance their lives while simultaneously upgrading yours as well. Some of your upgrades will be tangible. You may live in a better house, drive a better car or have more money in the bank than ever before. But I am here to tell you that the most valuable upgrades will be unseen. It will be the joy in your heart, the confidence in your soul, the happiness emanating from your presence and the wisdom oozing from your spirit. It will be total bliss.

This version of you is yearning to exist and contribute.

This level is waiting for you.

**It is time to unleash your full potential on the world.
Get ready for peak performance!**

Through the Eyes of the Lion

CHAPTER 3

DEVELOPING THE LION MENTATLITY

Developing the lion mentality is easier said than done. Every time I share this story people get excited. They make up their minds that they are going to be the lion. Some people put up posters of lions in their homes and offices, others change their social media pages to pictures of lions, and I've even seen some get a tattoo of a lion to show their commitment to this new mentality toward life. I love these reactions. It shows that the message is hitting people in the heart. They are responding with energy, drive, faith and excitement. It is awesome, but it is not enough.

I realize that in life it is not enough to want something, you must also know how to get it. You want to be the lion, not the gazelle. You make the decision, then what? As I continued to inspire thousands of people with this story I knew that I had to take it deeper if it was going to have a lasting impact. I did not want this to become a quick 'hype me up' moment. I needed to see lives changed more permanently. Inspired again by the Lion King, I found my answer.

Remember the beginning of the movie when Simba was talking to his father about the size of their kingdom. He told Simba that everywhere the light touches is our kingdom. Being driven by an uncontrollable and youthful curiosity, Simba asked about the shadowy place. We must never go there, Mufasa responded. This of course led Simba later decide to explore the mysterious shadowy lands. As expected, Simba found himself in inevitable danger by going into the shadowy place called the Elephant Graveyard. He brought Nala with him and Zazu (Mufasa's servant) followed them. They were chased and eventually cornered by the hyenas when Simba tried to make his presence known by his roar. He released a baby roar that did not strike an ounce of fear into the hyenas. Thankfully Mufasa came to the rescue unleashed an epic roar that sent shivers through the hyenas.

A lion's roar is significant. It distinguished them as the king of the jungle. Under the right conditions, a lion's roar can be heard up to 5 miles away. Developing your ROAR is also significant. You must let your presence be known in school, business or whatever industry you are involved with. People should feel your presence because you are constantly seeking ways to grow and become better. When you do then you will see amazing growth. This happened for Simba as well.

Powerful climatic ending. Simba walking up the mountain in the rain. Everyone looking on as he makes his climb to the top. As he reaches the top he pauses and hears Mufasa's voice once again "remember (who you are)" At that moment he takes his place and king and unleashes a mighty roar to show the world who he is.
We must do the same thing. We must develop our ROAR.

Take these four steps and use them repeatedly: R.O.A.R.

Raging hunger: Identify something you want and build your desire to have it. Ambition is key to the type of success that will make you fulfilled in life. When you have big goals and dreams in life then you are inspired to give big effort.

On the prowl: Prepare and position yourself to get the target goals that you desire in life. Greatness starts with desire, but it is aided by preparation. You cannot expect to live a great life unless you spend enormous amounts of time preparing for the things you want out of life. Without understanding what it is going to take to be successful, you will find yourself being disappointed too many times because you were not prepared. Remember this: The will to succeed is sustained by the will to prepare. You are not serious about success until you are 100% serious about preparation.

Attack your prey: Take aggressive action towards achieve the dreams and desires that you have identified and prepared for. You can talk about your dream all you want. You can prepare for your dream night and day. The magic happens when you take action. As a lion hunts its prey there is always that one special moment when it springs into action. When we take action it must be full of confidence and intentional effort. You will not stumble into greatness; you dreams will not come true on accident. It will be due to confident, intentional action from you.

Run with lions: Iron sharpens iron is a famous quote from the bible that teaches us to improve lives by improving the quality of people that we build relationships with. If you are ever going to be truly great, then you must develop relationships with other great people. This is the reason that I am creating a greatness movement that will create an environment for people to inspire each other to demand greatness and become the best version of themselves. When lions run with lions, greatness is on the horizon.

Be the Lion, not the Gazelle by working on your ROAR to demand greatness in your life.

Chapter 3 Summary Activity
How To Demand

❖ What percentage of your potential do you use on a daily basis?

_____

❖ Name three things you can do to maximize your potential consistently.

1. _____

2. _____

3. _____

❖ List the names of two people who see you as inspiration.

_____

_____

(*Share a word of encouragement with each person within the next 24 hours)

❖ List your DCMVP (Most Valuable Point/Principle) from this chapter.

_____

_____

❖ Why did this DCMVP stand out to you?

_____

_____

❖ How will you use this DCMVP to change your life?

_____

_____

Phase II: Performance
Maximizing Your Action

Performance is where my success is being developed by the process

This phase of demanding greatness requires an improved version of you. Your performance is what determines if you will live your dreams. Your performance will also impact how quickly you can achieve dreams. It is the evolutionary part of you. Your ability to perform under challenging situations will determine if you ever walk through the doors of possibility in your life.

Performance is the bridge between your potential and your possibilities in life.

The possibilities that exist in your life because of your potential can be made a reality through your performance.

Performance is all about execution. Getting the tasks done that need to be completed on your way to success. It brings your potential to life. People cannot see your potential until you make it visible and tangible with your performance.

Performance is a unique factor in this formula:

Potential + Performance = Possibilities

Potential is what you were equipped with when you were born. You did not select the gifts and talents you have, you discover them throughout your life. Possibilities exist because of the potential you possess. When it comes to performance, that factor in the formula is directly related to how much you decide commit yourself to greatness. This is where you have the ability to impact your life in an undeniable way.

Performance is always under your control. Nobody can make you do anything. They can influence you, but they cannot control you. You are not a robot that can be programmed. You are a human being with a mind that allows you to make decisions. This is the power of performance. It will always come down to you.

You will discover that there are things that can impact your performance. One of them is the environment around you. Your environment can empower you to do amazing things. You can flourish and blossom with amazing support, access to resources and the right people pushing you forward. On the flip side, a negative environment can be limiting. This story about the pumpkin illustrates my point flawlessly.

One day a farmer was walking through his pumpkin fields and happened to find a one-gallon glass jug. With nothing better to do, and finding himself in an experimental frame of mind, he poked a small pumpkin through the neck of the jug and left it. A year later, when the time came to harvest the pumpkins, the farmer again came across the glass jug. Oddly enough, the pumpkin had filled it completely and, with no more room to grow, had stopped growing. The farmer broke the glass and held a pumpkin that had assumed the exact size and shape of the jug.

Experts point out that people are like that pumpkin. They poke themselves into jugs beyond which they cannot grow. The difference here is that somebody else does not poke them into the jug — they do it themselves. Each of us decides how much we are going to grow and what kind of world we are going to live in.

We can only grow as large as the jug we're in — and we are the ones who decide its size and scope. The person who finds his world closing in around him, who finds it dull, routine, and uninteresting, has outgrown his "jug" and should start looking for a larger one.

Our environment can be like that jug, limiting our potential. Perhaps the pumpkin could have grown much larger, but the jug was defining the limits of growth. Make sure that you do not put yourself in environments that limit you. People will do that to you because they cannot see your potential. It is your responsibility to make sure that does not happen.

The way to make sure that your environment fits you as you grow throughout life is to take a lesson from the hermit crab. A friend shared an important lesson with me by using the hermit crab as an example. When a hermit crabs explores the world around them they are in search for hard shells to protect their fragile bodies. We essentially are doing the same thing in life. We are looking for supportive and protective environments and relationships to protect our growing dreams. When a hermit crab selects a shell there is one consistent characteristic in their choice. The shell must be too big for their bodies. You see, the hermit crab understands that it is not finished growing. Therefore, it must select a shell that is too large which automatically gives them room for growth. Once the hermit crabs grows to a point where that shell is no longer too big, it begins to search for a larger shell to transition into. They are always looking for bigger shells. We should do the same in our lives. Always look for bigger opportunities to grow, bigger stages to perform on and bigger places to express our unique abilities.

In chapters 4-6, I will discuss key factors that impact how we unleash peak performance. You will learn how to understand the importance of preparation, how to overcome failure and keys to developing winning habits that create the life you deserve. Evaluating and improving your performance will open doors of possibility in your life that will amaze you.

Chapter
4

Running The Race:
Knowing The Distance

"If you haven't confidence in self, you are twice defeated in the race
of life. With confidence you have won even before you started"
-Marcus Garvey

Knowing what to do is not enough to succeed in life. It is essential that you 'do what you know'. These two ideas are linked together in a way that will continually push you forward. The moment you commit to do what you know, then you are laying the foundation for growth and success.

I remember learning this lesson in my junior year of high school when I tried out for the football team. It was early February, that means it was fitness conditioning season for football players. When I showed up for tryouts I got quite a few skeptical looks and heard more than a few chuckles from current players. I cannot completely fault them for their doubts. As I walked through the door with my small 5'8, 135lb frame it was clear that I did not look like a football player.

I was there because I believe in not looking back on life with regrets. This was my last chance to try out and play high school football. I had to give it a shot or else I would not let myself rest peacefully about missing this opportunity. As practice started, we began running laps to get things flowing. My competitive nature was pushing me to prove myself. I did my best to keep up and stay in the front of the group. Then I started to notice fewer and fewer guys near the front with me. Next, even those who were near the front began to fade with fatigue. Considering that I was new and this was my first practice I could not help but to think that they knew something that I did not. I was concerned that they were holding back intentionally for reasons that I was unaware of. These were my thoughts, but none of them were true.

The truth is that they were all gassed and I was not. What I learned that day is that I was suited for a different sport. The football coach noticed this as well, that is why he introduced me to the track coach whose name was ironically, Coach Carter.

The very next day Coach Carter invited me to join the track team as a distance runner. He said I was a natural fit. I quickly gravitated to Coach Carter as a positive male role model. He provided me with a father figure that I did not have on a day to day basis with my father being in prison. He also taught me many valuable lessons.

When we attended our first track meet it was exciting. There were dozens of schools from all over the state of Michigan. There was a buzz of energy. Competitive juices were flowing. This was all new to me. I couldn't wait for my opportunity to get on the track and show what I could do. I wanted to see what I was made of. I embraced it all. I walked with pride in my green and gold Cody track suit. When it was time to race I ripped the suit off like I saw basketball players do in the NBA before their games. I thought I was the real deal. Our actual uniform was a thin white tank top and tight white track shorts with lose fitting green shorts over the top of the tighter shorts. Even in all of my excitement, I could not escape the jokes of friends and teammates who said that I looked like a black puff of smoke running around the track in those white uniforms. I felt so good that their jokes did not bother me. I was ready to run.

On your mark, get set, POW! The sound of the gun sent every runner lunging forward into the 1600m race also known as the one mile run. On an outdoor track, this consists of four laps around the track. Eager to know where I ranked, I finished the race and ran immediately to my coach. "Coach Carter, how did I do?" I said with bubbly excitement and eager anticipation. His response was shocking. He just looked at me. He had an odd expression on his face that was a mix of bewilderment and frustration. He went on to tell me that I should not be able to casually hold a conversation with him after running a mile in a competitive race. It was a sign that I ran the race the wrong way. I knew the distance of the race, but I did not know how to run that race properly.

Later on he told me that I had done something that he had not seen in his 20 plus years of coaching. I ran my first mile in less than five minutes and I ran the second half of the race faster than the first. Again, my youthful inexperience kicked in. I thought that was a good thing! He said it was not. It means that I did not give my all in the race. Once he said that, I realized that he was right. I did hold back. I conserved too much energy for the last lap. I did this out of fear. I had seen a few other runners earlier that day that were totally gassed on the track. Their bodies were so drained that it is almost like they were walking on the track, in slow motion, and in quick sand. There were people in the stands laughing at how hard they were trying to run and how slow their bodies were moving. I quickly decided, that will not be me.

My mistake is a common one. I made a plan based on my fears, not my goals. I encourage you to learn from my lesson. Plan to achieve what you want, not what you want to avoid. I did not learn my lesson overnight. There were many track meets where I had to avoid Coach Carter because I knew I had done it again. My times were getting better, but I was still not giving my all. I had formed a bad habit that was reinforced every time I saw the struggling runner guy being laughed. In addition, I became fascinated with the exhilaration of zooming past other runners on my last lap because I saved so much of my energy from earlier in the race.

The biggest frustration Coach Carter had with me was my lack of vision for what I could achieve. One day he took me into the gym and pointed at the schools records for track and field. It listed the best all time performances by Cody athletes. He brought my attention to one name: William Hill. He held the school record for the mile with a time of 4 minutes 20 seconds. Coach Carter told me that he felt I had the talent to challenge the record but that it would never happen if I did not stop sandbagging the middle laps of the mile.

Then came the day I decided to take Coach Carter up on his challenge. It was the state qualifying track meet. I was pumped up with excitement. I always ran my best times on the road away from Cody. Part of me wants to say it was because of the energy of competing against people from all over the state or region; but another part always reminds me that we were running on a concrete track at Cody. Needless to say that did not help us out at all.

The day started out well. I posted a PB (personal best) in my first race of the day which was the 800m run. I ran the first leg of the 3200m relay, we called in the 4x8. My time was 2minutes 2 seconds, only 3 seconds from my goal of breaking the 2 minute mark. I felt good, today was my day to finally give it my all in that 1600m run. When the time came I blasted out of the gate and put myself into the top 3 running positions. I did not want to be first because that is considered the 'rabbit' position of the race. I kept my position through the second lap without a problem. Things were going good. My problem traditionally was always the third lap. That was the lap that I usually choose to coast so that I could save energy for the final lap. Well on that day I went for it.

My third lap was just as strong as the 2nd lap. I was in prime position going into the last lap, but my body was confused. It was like my body started talking to me.

"Hey man, uh what are you doing to me?"

"Did we just run all the laps with full effort?"
"Who does that?"
"What does this even mean?"
"Wait, there's ANOTHER lap to go"
"I just don't understand this?"

My inner conversation was hilarious. My body was not comprehending what I was doing and eventually my mind joined in on the fun. As I ran the back stretch of the final lap I started feeling the effects of giving my best effort. That back stretch looked so long that I thought it was a mile all by itself. I decided that I was going to just close my eyes for a quick second to see if that would help. After a few strides I looked up and it didn't work. It was just as long as before and my body was just as tired. I started feeling muscles get sore that I didn't even know I had. But through it all I kept pushing, kept my legs churning and kept my pace. I finished that race with another PB. To date, it is the fastest I've ever run the mile; I posted a 4:37. That's far off the record that Coach Carter envisioned for me, but it showed me what I had been missing all that time. The will do give my all and run the race without fear.

Now let me tell you, giving your all will come with a cost. When I finished that race it felt like somebody set off a fire in my chest. I felt violated. Who would do something like this to me? The attendants were trying to give me water but I kept waving them off. All I wanted to do was lay down, right there on the grass. That's a terrible idea by the way, but you couldn't tell me otherwise in that moment. Eventually I fell to the ground in complete exhaustion. The faithful attendant still found a way to put a cup of water in my hand which did help to cool the fire burning in my chest slightly.

This experience taught me that sometimes you have to compete with the best to unleash your best. It was not a coincidence that I gave my personal best in both races on the day of state qualifying rounds. The tough thing for me was that I was also scheduled to run two more races. On competition days, coach usually had me run the 3200m relay, 1600m run, 800m run and 3200m run. That's four distance running events in one day. I did it all the time, but not at this level. I guess you could say that was another reason I didn't put it all on the track in each race. I knew that I had a long day ahead of me. Other schools, like Cass Technical High School for example, had a rotation of runners. No guy on their team ran more than two events in a day. I would often be leaning over in exhaustion from a race while looking at one of them chilling, getting ready to face me in the next race with fresh legs.

One last lesson that giving my all taught me was both symbolic and practical. Up until that day, I would always 'dry heave' after every race. A 'dry heave' is when your body is trying to vomit but nothing is coming out because my stomach was empty. It was so bad that I would not eat anything at least 4-6 hours before my events. If I did then it was coming back up. My teammates would watch me finish a race, head for the bathroom and start shouting, "Aye, there goes Earl!" They got a good laugh out of my situation every time. There was a great lesson that I learned from finally giving my all that day. Giving your all can sometimes eliminate problems that have been nagging at you. After that day where I gave my all, I never had to dry heave or vomit after a race again. My assistant track coach said it was like my body was waiting all that time for me to finally leave it all on the track.

When you decide to finally give your all things in your life will become different. Old problems will face and new opportunities will emerge.

One major mistake that I have seen people make in their pursuit of success is relying only on what they know. They believe that knowing is key to their success. However, as I once heard a wise man say: That is not incorrect, but it is incomplete. I want you to know that the saying is true, "knowledge is power"; but as GI Joe taught me knowing is only half the battle.

I cannot tell you how many times I have sat with a client and listened to them say how they know what to do only to watch them fail to do it. One of those times happened recently as I was coaching a man who was returning to college after spending some time away from school due to poor grades his first time around. On that day, his passion was palpable. His energy was contagious. His personality filled the room. This guy was excited about life, happy to have a second chance and seemingly ready to succeed. When I asked what would make this time differently he responded by saying, "This time I know what to do". My response was direct:

Life is not about knowing what to do; it is about doing what you know.

By the time you reach this phase of the journey in life you know most of what you need to know in order for you to succeed in creating progress toward the life you want to live.

- You know that you should spend time aligning your life with your spiritual beliefs.
- You know that family comes first.
- You know that you must invest time into your marriage or relationship.
- You know that you should consistently save and invest your money.
- You know that healthy eating habits can improve and save your life.
- You know that exercise will strengthen your body.
- You know that you need to study in order to do well in school.
- You know that your success on the job requires more commitment.

In this performance phase of life we are not rewarded simply for our ability, but for our consistency. Here the value of potential begins to shrink and the emphasis on execution rises like never before. No longer will flashes of potential greatness be enough. You will need to sustain greatness. This happens when you discover ways to improve your performance in a way that will empower you to repeat it when new opportunities come into your life.

The issue is not that you are unaware of what to do; the issue is that you have not found the compelling reasons that will drive you through hell and back to do it. You must find strong enough reasons to push you past complacency and mediocrity into success. You need reasons that inspire you to go above and beyond the call of duty. These reasons should be planted so deep in your heart, so entrenched in your soul, that no adversity can ever uproot it out of you. Once you have reached this level of commitment then you will easily understand that life is not about knowing what to do. It is nearly all about doing what you know, with this understanding: as you do more of what you know, what you know will continue to grow. Knowledge is key. Application of knowledge is linked to acquisition of knowledge. Do more and you will know more. Know more and you will grow more. Once this happens, progress indeed will be yours.

Running the race has many lessons here are a few helpful points that I have learned:

- o There are a crowd of witnesses: Two groups of people. Those who doubt you and those who believe in you. One group is confident that you will fail. The other group is convinced that you will succeed. One of those groups will be wrong. Be sure to disappoint the right group.

- o Lay aside every weight: What holds you back from becoming your best and delivering a peak performance? Identify those things and eliminate them from your life.

- o Run the race with patience: Your strategy must include the entire race. The part of the race that you are in right now is just that, a part of the race. You will need to take a longer term view of the race to best decide what you should be your next step.

- o That is set before us: In track and field, running in someone else's lane is a violation for a lot of events. We must understand that the path set before us is custom made for our success. Trust the process and stay focused on what belongs to you o   Looking unto God: You must have a laser focus on the ultimate goal of your race. Why are you running your race? For you, if the reason is religious, be true to that. If it is not then clearly define what it is for you. Be clear on why you are running the race. Mission breathes energy into YOU as you pursue purpose.

o   Who for the joy set before him endured the cross, despising the shame and is set down at the right hand of the throne: You will be drawn forward for the purpose of winning the race. There will be obstacles that affect you as well as people who try to shame, discourage or embarrass you. However none of that can stop you from taking your rightful place in victory in your race.

Know the distance, prepare for the journey and be convinced that you have what it takes to finish.

Through the Eyes of the Lion

CHAPTER 4

DEVELOPING THE LION MENTATLITY

The lion's mentality is superior is many ways. A very significant way this is demonstrated is through the sense of control that comes from planning. A person with a plan has an edge of the person who only knows how to respond to life as they go along. When it comes to the hunter and the hunted, it is easy to understand that only one planned to be in that situation.

The lion takes on the role of the hunter which allows it to dictate the terms of the hunt. The lion's decision to pounce is the signal that triggers the gazelle to begin running. The gazelle has no input on when this process begins. The gazelle cannot run even choose the direction that it wants to run until after it knows where the lions are coming from. Also the gazelle cannot decide when the hunt is over. It must keep running until safety is absolutely secured.

This is the benefit that planning will give to you. It empowers you to map out the direction, speed and destination of your efforts in life. The key is to understand is that it requires internal motivation to be in control of this process. Remember that the lion's hunger and desire is what makes it decide to take action. On the other hand the gazelle has to wait and respond. This is no way to life a fulfilled life. Unfortunately too many people find themselves in this position. Their life if controlled by outside factors like other people's opinions, urgent deadlines and limited resources.

Developing the lion mentality will require for you to consistently increase your knowledge and awareness. A wise and experienced lion will know all the tendencies of its prey. Similarly, you must understand all the details about the goals and plans that you have for your life. As a speaker one of the most important things I have to think about is the needs of my audience. This factor changes every time I stand in front of a crowd. As I speak to business owners and professionals, I understand the need to address their concerns about their company. It allows me to be analytical and go in depth with my talk. When I speak to athletes, I must use my knowledge of the audience to change the direction of my speech. The urgency and energy level is different because the competition is more tangible and always on display for others to see. Speaking to youth is similar, they often require more catchy quotes and vivid examples. If I do not have a strong knowledge base about my audience then my plan to succeed is automatically weakened. The same is true for the goal and plan you have for yourself. You must continually gather information and knowledge that helps you to create a plan for the success you desire.

Be the Lion, not the Gazelle by planning out what you need to do to become successful.

Chapter 4 Summary Activity
Running the Race: Knowing the Distance

❖ Coaching is Key: Who are your current coaches or mentors

_____

_____

❖ Name someone who you would like to become a future coach or mentor

_____

_____

❖ Expanding Your Knowledge Base: What new activity will help you to grow your knowledge base?

_____

_____

❖ What new organizations or groups can you join to expand your accountability to apply your knowledge?

_____

_____

❖ List your DCMVP (Most Valuable Point/Principle) from this chapter.

_____

_____

❖ Why did this DCMVP stand out to you?

_____

_____

❖ How will you use this DCMVP to change your life?

_____

_____

Chapter
5

Coming In 2nd Place: I tried my best but...

"Use your successful moments to build confidence and your challenging moments to build character" -Anonymous

Every successful achiever has come face-to-face with failure. That failure can take on many forms. The most critical thing is knowing how to respond properly to the failures you face. You can either go through your failures or you can grow through your failures.

Going through failure places your focus on surviving the experience. It is like living to see another day. That is something positive about going through your failures. It is a sign that you are refusing to allow failure to stop you from pursuing success.

Growing through failure is even better. It places your focus on becoming better because of the experience. There is a famous saying, 'What doesn't kill me, only makes me stronger.' I believe this to be true. It becomes more powerful when you intentionally focus on ways that you can become stronger from each situation you face.

These life defining moments of growing through failure will position you for success beyond your expectations.

One of the hardest lessons to learn and fully understand is that your personal best may not be 'the best'. There are times where someone else's best effort is better than yours. This can be a hard pill to swallow, but you must continue to strive to give your best regardless of the outcome. Use these moments to learn ways to improve your performance. I love the quote by St. Jerome when he said,

"Good, better, best. Never let it rest. 'Til your good is better and your better is best"

The lesson is this: Your best can get better. Even if someone else is better in that moment, you can learn from the experience. This will help you to prepare for future moments. You cannot let losing defeat you. Let me say that again clearly. Losing does not have to defeat you. There are lessons to be learned from losing. Those lessons can help you to make changes and adjustments that will lead you to victory in future situations.

Nothing gets your attention quite like a painful loss. The sting of losing never feels good, but the joy of winning is worth the risk. Remember this 2nd is on the way to first. Winnings is a process that will include losing at different points of the experience. At one point you were not a number in the race at all. Every professional starts out as an amateur. Even the experts have had to deal with their difficult moments in the process of becoming great at what they do.

Recently I had to deal with losing in the process of pursing a major goal. In 2008, I joined a group called Toastmasters International. Toastmasters International is a world leader in communication and leadership development. They have more than 330,000 members. Members improve their speaking and leadership skills by attending one of the more than 15,000 clubs in 135 countries that make up our global network of meeting locations. Needless to say, this is a good organization.

Lead by the encouragement of a few Toastmasters within my club I decided to compete in the Toastmasters International Speech Competition. At this time I had only been a member for one year, so I still felt new to the organization. However, the overwhelming support that I received from my club pushed me forward with confidence. The smiles and mentorship of Merv Jersak, Bil Moore, Tracey Maroney, Tim Bey and many others encouraged me.

There are six rounds of the international speech contest. The club level, division level, area level, district level, semifinals and finals. I was nervously excited before the first round at the club level. Our club is one of the toughest in our area so I knew the competition would be stiff. Thankfully I finished first and moved on to the next round. At the division level I also finished in first place which moved me to the area level. The area level completion was noticeable more challenging as I watched other speakers. I knew it would require the best I had within in, which is exactly what I delivered. My first place finish gave me the opportunity to compete for the District 62 competition in Battle Creek, Michigan. Winning the District speech competition means that speaker would be ranked #1 of all the speakers from 87 different clubs all over the state of Michigan.

That day was exciting. I drove to the event full of confidence and ready to deliver. When my time came, I gave the best edition of my speech that I had ever given. The outcome was clear to me and when they announced, "First place speaker, DeAndre Carter". I was overflowing with excitement. It was a "mama we made it" type of moment where you are proud of what you've done along with all of your friends and family. I was floating on cloud nine. Here I was in my first speech competition and I had won my first 4 rounds! As I stood on that stage, trophy in hand, I realized that I was only 2 more victories away from the illustrious title of "World Champion of Public Speaking".

The next step was to get ready for an even higher level of competition in the semifinal round. One day while sitting in my office preparing my next speech I received a phone call from my club president. When she spoke to me I recognized that tone of her voice was completely void of excitement. I didn't know what was wrong, but I do know I was not prepared at all for what she was about to say next. "DeAndre, I'm sorry but you have been disqualified from the International Speech competition effective immediately". Wow! I was stunned. I could not understand what was happening. She went on to explain that I was not listed as an official member of the club at the time the contest started. This stunned me even more. I had been attending meetings and paying dues for months before the contest began. That is when she explained that a clerical error by one of our club officers led to the disqualification. She promised me that she would appeal and fight on my behalf, which she did, in vain. Toastmasters International upheld its decision. They ruled that the letter of the policy is greater than the spirit of the policy. I was left devastated to say the least.

Fast forward to last year, March 2015. It had been years since my disqualification from the international speech competition. Many life events has occurred within my life during that time period. I was married, had a child, divorced, evicted, had my car repossessed, co-founded an organization, left that organization, started several businesses and started writing this book. Through all of that, I never forgot about my desire to enter the speech competition again. It never left me how my last attempt ended. I always wondered what would have happened if given the chance to keep going. I convinced myself that I had to give it another shot.

During my second attempt to win the title of World Champion, I was again successful at earning a victory during my first three rounds. It was exciting all over again, but felt so much different since I was more familiar with the process. Also the structure of the contest was different. This time the semifinal and final rounds would be held that the Toastmaster International World Convention which was being held at the Caesars Palace in Las Vegas! Earning a victory at the District level carried more weight this time around. It would mean punching a ticket to Vegas to compete against speakers from all over the world.

Less than four days before the District competition I had someone ask me a question. She said, "How do you feel about knowing your competition?" I smiled and said I like knowing everything I can. Then she shared that the previous year's District winner was also competing again. This perked my ears and stroked my competitive fire. I couldn't wait to get home and google him. I found that not only did he win the previous year, but he had won 4 of the past 7 years. While this might have intimidated some, it inspired me. I knew that I had to bring my A+ game. I dug in even deeper in my preparation. I reviewed my speech to make sure every syllable, every gesture, and every word was meaningful. This was like trying to beat the Spurs in basketball or Patriots in football. I was competing against a proven winner.

I arrived to the District competition hours early to size up the room and prepare my mind for victory. I took the stage, with the room empty, and delivered my speech with power. I took pictures with the trophy that I expected to take home with me. I meditated and imagined them calling my name as the first place winner. Today was going to be my day.

One of the key moments in every speech contest is the drawing for the order of speakers. I always prefer going last because it allows me to see all other speakers before I deliver mine. I have always been able to feed off the energy and live up to a big moment. That day there were 7 speakers and I drew the number 6. Not bad, I knew that I would be able to hear every other speaker except one before I spoke. As I asked around, trying to see who had the final spot I found that it was the previous year's winner. Wow, the one person who I wanted to see for sure would be going after me. I knew that I only had one choice. Set the bar high enough that it would be difficult for him to clear it and take home victory.

While the other speakers were delivering their messages, it became clear to me that I had a very good chance at making my dream a reality. I had been visualizing Vegas for months. I changed my

Facebook cover photo to a picture of the Caesars' Palace the moment I decided to compete. I was chomping at the bit waiting for my chance to deliver. When my time came I did just that! Things were going well, a little too well actually.

One of the biggest rules in the Toastmasters speech competition is timing. You are allowed 5-7 minutes to deliver your speech with a 30 second cushion on each side of the time allotment. That means 4:29 or 7:31 gets an automatic disqualification, no questions asked! Well, as I was speaking the red light came on. This signaled that I had reached the 7 minute mark and had less than 30 seconds to conclude my speech. I was having so much fun that I had not even started the conclusion to my speech! How was this happening? All of my timed rehearsals were less than 6 minutes alone and less than 6:30 with a live audience! The challenge was to bring my speech to a strong, powerful close without sounding rushed and definitely before the 7:30 mark. I calmly finished my point, recalculated my conclusion in my head on the spot and gave a condensed but exciting versions of the conclusion. When I was finished I could only think about one thing, did I finish within time? Of course the winner from the previous year was still due to speak. At that moment I knew there were two hurdles between me and Vegas; my time and his speech. Listening to him was a treat. He is a great speaker. He set up him punch lines well. His diction was matchless. His poised and self-confidence were palpable. I watched intently comparing his performance to mine in my head. Once I saw the green light indicating that he had reached the 5 minute mark, I thought to myself 'unless he pulls out some back flips and splits, I've got him beat with my speech today'. Whether right or wrong, that's how I felt. Now I was both excited and nervous. Excited because I felt that I had delivered a District winning speech; nervous because I still did not know if it was within time. The last thing I needed in my life was another disqualification from the international speech competition. Only this time the fault would be all mine.

I can tell you that he did not perform any back flips or splits to conclude his speech. I felt confident that I was in good position for the win. Next we waited as the judges tallied their scores. During this time contestants are interviewed in front of the crowd to buy time for vote counting. One of the vote counters was someone that I knew. As we were being interviewed the vote counters walked into the room. While I knew she could not signal or say anything about the results (especially with me standing in the front of the room), I was studying her body language for clues. I saw one clue that concerned me. She made no contact with anyone. She kept her head down. I interpreted that as bad news. I kept thinking, oh no I might be disqualified again. As the speakers were asked to return to their seats I readied myself for the outcome.

The host calmly said before we share the results, I have an announcement to make. There were no disqualifications for time. All speakers were within time. I almost jumped up out of my seat! What a sigh of relief. I knew that didn't guarantee me victory, but at least my experience would not end in another disqualification. They announced the third place speaker, it wasn't me. They announced the second place speaker, again it wasn't me (it was the previous year's winner). Then came the moment, "And the winner of today's speech contest, representing District 62 in Las Vegas this fall….DeAndre Carter!"

The stage was set. I had two months to prepare for Vegas and I used them well. I travelled all over the city and state speaking to groups and getting feedback. All of the evaluations and feedback sessions were immeasurably helpful, including one where there were over 100 people witnessing a no holds barred critique of my work. That evaluation was delivered by a one of the past Toastmaster world champions. Other evaluation sessions went deep into the night and challenged my will, as well as my coachable attitude. When it was all said and done I had invested countless hours preparing for an opportunity that I had dreamed about for years. I was ready to take flight to Vegas and make history by becoming the first speaker from the state of Michigan to win the World Championship of Public Speaking from Toastmasters International in the 75 year history of the contest.

When I arrived in Vegas I was locked in. The environment was big and my expectations were even bigger. I came with one purpose, one goal, and one thing in my sight: becoming World Champion.

Saving the best for last.
Welcome to round 10.

Walking into the dress rehearsals was a bit of a surreal moment. I found the area where my assigned round would be gathering. Here I was about to put faces to the names that I had been seeing for months. Again, we were representing Japan, Canada, Nigeria and six different states from the US. There was nothing but smiles and positive energy flowing from the people in our group. One guy, Michael Williams II, caught my attention in a unique way. He shared a quote that made me reply, "Man, that goods. Sounds familiar" He laughed and said, "It should, I heard it from you on one of your YouTube videos!"

I cannot say enough about the people I met that evening. We kept each other in high spirits the entire time. I remember giving high fives and pumping everybody up back stage before it was time to deliver. Joe Grondin's smile was magnetic. Emmanuael Fadahunsi had a youthful and contagious energy. Brian Olds was friendly, but focused and on a mission. Mike Carr was seasoned, I could tell he was prepared.

Again as I watched each speaker, my confidence was high. I led off a red-hot round of speaking. Everyone who stepped on stage did so with an obviously level of preparation and expectation. I was excited for everybody. In our short time together we learned to support each other despite being competitors for the chance to speak in the finals on the world stage.

While votes were being tallied, we were all called back to the stage for brief interview. My response to a question allowed me to inspire the crowd using a brief version of the Lion v Gazelle story. My day was going great! Once all speakers had been interviewed it was time for us to head to our seats for the announcement of the 3 speakers from our round.

The time had come. All of the rehearsals, evaluations, travelling and long nights was about to pay off. "Coming in third place tonight is

Nelson Ortega." "Next, coming in second place is Naoki Tamura." Wow, I was really feeling excited now. I knew I was about the live the moment that I had rehearsed in my mind for months. "Tonight's winner, advancing to the final round of the 2015 International Speech Competition is…..Joseph Grondin!" As the room erupted in celebratory congratulations, I was again stunned. Not only did I not win first, I didn't even place within my round. I thought I had done so well. My best wasn't good enough on that night. Of course, the professional within me found Nelson, Naoki and Joe to congratulate them all. Once that was done I made a direct path to my hotel room to gather my thoughts. The loss was heart wrenching.

Multiple contest coordinators mentioned our round as the most difficult and challenging from what they had seen earlier in the day. I must say that I fully agree. I thought my fellow round 10 members all represented themselves well. When I returned to Michigan I had a lot of people asking if I thought I could have done a better job. My honest answer is no. I delivered a great speech, but the judges felt others were better. That part is out of my control. I jokingly say I wrote a great paper, but not the one the teacher was looking for. As I prepare for this year's contest I take away what I learned and expect to do even better on my next attempt.

Looking back on my experience I recognize that I did not win the world title, but I still walked away from the event feeling like a winner. There were some things I did win during the event. I won the respect of my peers. I remain in contact with several of them as we encourage each other to become better speakers. I won the opportunity to meet and network with past world champions of public speaking like Jim Key, Randy Harvey and Lance Miller. I won a trip to a city that I had never visited before. I won the support of Toastmasters from all over the state of Michigan who were rooting for my success. My experience taught me that it is possible to draw winning lessons from a losing experience.

The speech I delivered along this amazing roller coaster journey is titled, RISE. It was inspired by an MSU first generation freshman student from Kalamazoo, Michigan. The experience of helping her to bounce back from adversity to live her dreams will always be memorable for me. I want to share the speech with you so its message can inspire you as well.

RISE

Have you ever one of those moments where life simply feels perfect. The sun is shining, the birds are chirping, your heart is singing....life is just grand and suddenly ...WHAM!

You encounter another moment. A moment that snatches your breath away, a moment that makes your heart drop, a moment that puts your mind in a state of disbelief and brings tears to your eyes, a moment too heavy to carry, leaving you only with enough energy to stumble to your knees.

Madam Toastmaster, fellow toastmasters and anyone who has ever had a difficult moment in life.

It is in these during these tough times, what I call defining moments, that you must find the strength to RISE!

These are the special moments in life where you take hold of the unique opportunity to experience a monumental shift in a new direction. In these moments you must realize that success is yours the moment you decide to RISE.

I will never forget the day she walked into my advising office with a look on her face of complete desperation, overwhelming helplessness but, yet still a glimmer of hope.

Her name is Brittany. At the time she was a struggling freshman at Michigan State University. She was the first person in the history of her family to attend college. Her second semester was beginning to look like her first, where she received a disappointing 1.1 grade on a 4.0 scale. She was at risk of losing her scholarship, and her dream along with it. She was at risk of being forced to leave the university. She was face to face with a defining moment in her life disguised as......a setback.

Have YOU ever felt like that? Have you ever had an experience that took so much out of you that you did not know if you had what it takes to simply continue moving forward?

If you can relate then I have news for you tonight. It may have been your first time, *but it will not be your last* so I will share with you the insight that has guided me throughout the darkest days of my life and carried Brittany through the rough waters of her college years.

Rise to the occasion
Rise to the challenge
Rise to seize the defining moment that is right in front you

As Brittany had a simple response, "DeAndre, how do I RISE?" Perhaps that same question is in the room tonight.

So in response I simply say, follow the letters let them lead the way, REMEMBER.

Remember a time where you were your best because it makes you feel good.

Remember when you were so confident that you felt like you were the template for success, in life.

Or remember when you saw at that special somebody, and from across the room and thought to yourself. "Before YOU SAY YES, first let me ask the question, "Would you like to go out to dinner with me?"

These moments are necessary; they allow you to empower yourself for what is next.

Remembering allows you to INSPIRE.

Inspire yourself to take the next step. The next step toward your dreams, the next step toward your goals, the next step toward success. Inspire, the opposite of expire, means to breathe life into. Take a deep breath with me. Just like that you can take a moment to breathe life into your dreams, into your relationships, into the lives of your family members and those you love most.

But also…

Never forget the power of a question. I remember when I went for a big goal and a friend asked, DeAndre what it you fail…again? Dude, that's not inspirational.

Instead of that question, today I want you to ask yourself, What if it works? What if I do my best? What if I do everything I can and things actually begin to work in my favor instead of working against me?

Once inspired, you will be empowered to SHIFT.

Shift your focus upward when life tries to pull you down. For Brittney the challenge to stay focused was tested consistently as she carried the weight of her entire family's hopes and dreams on her petite shoulders. Things were improving for her when life decided to add to the situation when her apartment caught fire and destroyed nearly everything she owned. But Brittany responded like a true champion with a fire of her own. The winds of adversity only served to fan the flames of desire that burned deep within her.

Her focus allowed her to EXPECT.

Expect the best in life. Expect to win. Winners can see the victory before it happens. I agree with Albert Einstein when he said, "Imagination is everything. It is a preview of life's coming attractions". Time spent worrying what will happen if I lose is a form of preparation to lose. Winning does not happen by mistake. It happens within the framework of great expectations.

In Brittany's case her expectations along with my coaching fueled her turnaround. Not only did she keep her scholarship, not only did she avoid being kicked out of school, but she decided to put an exclamation point on her defining moment by earning a 3.6 grade on that 4.0 scale during the semester of her defining moment. And the best part of it all for me, was having the privilege to meet an awesome person like Brittany. A woman with the strength to live her dreams even in the face of her fears. You have the same opportunity available to you.

Fellow Toastmasters and welcomed guests, when you encounter your next defining moment. A moment where you are not sure of the outcome. A moment where life offers you an opportunity to experience a monumental shift in a new direction, never forget success is yours. As you remember when you were at your best, as you inspire yourself to take the next step, as you shift your focus upward when life tries to pull you down, and as you expect to win then you too will be able to rise to the occasion, you too will be able to rise to the challenge and you too will be able to rise and seize the defining moment that is waiting just for you!

I have come here to remind you that success is yours the moment you decide to RISE!

This speech will always have a special place in my heart. The idea of standing tall in the face of fear and adversity is empowering. It reminds me that life does have painful moments, but we can push past the pain. Being able to find the strength to push past the pain happens best when you focus on your purpose. The story below always reminds me of the powerful connection between pain and purpose.

Pain from failure can become power when it is mixed with purpose.

I read a story where a 12 year old boy watched his mother grow ill. He went with her to see the physician who gave them news mixed mostly despair, but also with a glimmer of hope. The doctor told them that he would love to treat the mother for her illness but he could not do so until the sun rose in the morning to provide the light necessary to apply the treatment. That little boy fervently prayed through the night, "Please God, let my mother live until the sun comes up so the doctor can save her". With tears pouring down his face the little boy held on to hope, but it would not be enough. His mother passed in the darkness of the night. Her death became as a driving force in his quest to create a way for light to exist in darkness. This is one of the reasons that Thomas Edison willed his way through more than 1000 failed attempts to create the light bulb. Pain can be used for a greater purpose when you allow it to inspire you to greatness.

Demanding Greatness involves learning how to pull out winning lessons from losing experiences.

Through
the
Eyes
of the
Lion

CHAPTER 5

DEVELOPING THE LION MENTATLITY

Demanding greatness requires a unique type of mental toughness. Regardless of the career path you have chosen, you will be tested by failure. Lawyers lose cases they labored over. Athletes lose games they trained for. Entrepreneurs lose customers that took years to gain. Executives lose accounts to their competitors. Students fail exams despite studying all night. Actors/actresses lose roles they auditioned for. And lions fail to catch every gazelle the chase.

They fail more often that you make think. In fact, out of every 10 tries the lion only successfully catches a gazelle 3 times. What happens on the other 7 attempts? The lion gives everything they have knowing that it is possible for them to not get what they want. This possibility of failure does not stop them from hunting. The key is mental toughness. Failure to catch the gazelle did not eliminate the hunger burning inside them. As a result, they make the important decision to try again. They recover, prepare and eventually pursue another hunt. They do not give up and neither should you.

The day I found out how many tries it takes a lion to catch a gazelle literally changed my life. It was not a new lesson to me; but it did add a new layer of truth to my understanding about overcoming adversity. The lion is king of the jungle, they know it and so does every other animal in the jungle. Their confidence is sure and their position is firm. However, this does not come without a test. They do not win every battle, but they do not let that stop them from chasing the things that they want. Failure will test your resolve. It will challenge your belief and force you to decide how your respond when things do not go your way.

As I explained in this chapter, I did not win the World Championship of public speaking like I intended. This became a major test for me. I licked my wounds and began chasing another goal, another gazelle. How do you respond when you fail to achieve your goals? Do you doubt your talents and abilities? Do you fall into a funk or feel depressed? Do you hide and cower away from future opportunities? The answers to these questions are important to your future.

Tomorrow's reality relies on today's faith. Not only must give go still pursue your goals after failure, but you must go after them with complete confidence that you will achieve them. You cannot afford to allow the residue of doubt to contaminate your performance. Use your shortcomings as inspiration to make sure they never happen again. In your toughest moments you must find the strength to believe even in the face of failure.

Be the Lion, not the Gazelle by standing tall in the face of failure with faith that you will only get better each time you try.

Chapter 5 Summary Activity
Coming In 2nd Place: I Tried My Best But...

❖ List a time where you felt like you failed (fell short of your expectations).

_____

_____

❖ What did you learn from this process?

_____

_____

❖ Have you used that lesson to improve your life? (performance)

_____

_____

❖ How will you use this lesson to help you live your dream?

_____

_____

❖ List your DCMVP (Most Valuable Point/Principle) from this chapter.

_____

_____

❖ Why did this DCMVP stand out to you?

_____

_____

❖ How will you use this DCMVP to change your life?

_____

_____

Chapter
6

How To Win: Unleashing Peak Performance

"You were born to win, but to be a winner, you must plan to win, prepare to win, and expect to win" –Zig Ziglar

Winning is born from a burning desire to outperform yourself. The highest level of winning is not only about beating the competition. It is about realizing that you are your only competition.

Winning is a process that forms character within you. This is process grooms you for greater goals, hones you for a hopeful future and inspires you to create new dimensions of excellence on a daily basis. Knowing how to win in one area of life automatically equips you to understand how to win in other areas of life.

I am excited to share some winning strategies that have impacted my life:

Diamond Time

There are seasons where you must seize your moment if you want to take your life to the next level. One of the most important opportunities in my life was being accepted to Michigan State. I knew how this could change my life and help me to become a trailblazer in my family. I also knew that I would need to do things differently if I wanted different results in my life.

The best habit I started in college was reading books that challenged my thinking. One day while shopping in Target I saw a book titled, "It Only Takes A Minute To Change Your Life" by Willie Jolley. The title caught my attention quickly. I remember thinking if it only takes a minute to change my life then what am I doing wrong. I had been trying to change my life for years. The idea that Willie Jolley shared in the book was in fact life changing. He said, "The minute to decide to go after your dreams is the minute you change your life." I agree, his book helped me to see how I could my time, my minutes, to create the life of my dreams. In the book he quotes Mike Murdock saying that we all have 24 box cars given to each day. Do you fill them with dirt or diamonds? It was at that moment that every day I needed to invest what I call "Diamond Time!"

Diamond time is when you invest effort today that will reward you in the future. I challenge you every day to invest some diamond time into your dreams. You cannot afford to let a day go by without making some progress toward your dreams.

I have been sharing this idea at MSU for years and now I am sharing it with the world. Diamond time helped me to become a first generation college graduate because I was willing to make sacrifices to achieve success. I used fun as a reward for doing my work. If there was a party or event I wanted to attend then I knew that I had to get some work done to 'earn' my fun time. When I was becoming exhausted I scheduled time to rest. Since I was aware of my disadvantaged background I worked hard to balance the scales. I read books and developed relationships to shorten my learning curve. As I grew to learn more about motivational speaking I decided to invest diamond time in connecting with some of my idols and mentors. I have had the privilege of meeting Tony Robbins, Les Brown, that late great Zig Ziglar, Eric Thomas, Willie Jolley, Otis Williams and many others. Each one of them made a deposit of diamond time into my life that has stuck with me.

- Tony Robbins told me to keep giving to others and always find ways to keep working on my craft.
- Les Brown encouraged me to remember that I'm too blessed to be stressed.
- The late great Zig Ziglar said I must stay genuine in my motives, always focus on helping others.
- Eric Thomas this nugget: There is no such thing as a bad day, only bad moments that we allow to grow into bad days.
- Willie Jolley greeted me with a big smile saying, "You must be DeAndre Carter" before sharing invaluable insight about creating success as a professional speaker.
- Otis Williams watched me for the first time and said, "You're good! Normally when somebody asks me to hear them speak I'm thinking we've got work to do, but with you I'm thinking we've got something to work with here."

Diamond Time equips you with the ability to produce in crunch time.

Diamond Time has a certain look to it. Every great achievement comes along with a story about how much time was invested by the achiever. College graduates have stories about pulling all-nighters for the big exam. The best of the best can often be found pouring themselves into their work. Hours upon hours in the library, reading books, performing research and writing papers. Diamond time attracts degrees.

Entertainers push themselves to the limits to rise to the top. During one stretch of time, entertainment icon Beyoncé put in 18 hour days for two straight weeks, filming 14 videos in the process. Staffers were in awe of her ability to still be the most energetic person on set despite her lack of sleep. This did not happen by accident. Beyoncé had been preparing for greatness years before she became a household name. As a teen she had a routine where she would run for miles while singing lyrics in an attempt to build her stamina. Beyoncé has put in her diamond time in ways that have separated her from the crowd.

Politicians who desire to become presidential candidates know that their will and stamina are certain to be tested. During his successful bid for reelection, President Barack Obama had a month that included 45 campaign visits, 12 rallies in 12 different states, 7 fundraisers, 3 talk show appearances, 3 presidential debates all while travelling 23,000 miles in the process. President Obama put in the required diamond time to make history in becoming the first African American to be elected as President of the United States of America and then again for his reelection.

Athletes invest countless hours to become the best in their sport. Can you imagine how many times Kobe Bryant has shot a basketball in his lifetime? Kobe is known for his tremendous work ethic and 4am practice sessions. One night after a loss to the Miami Heat, he decided that he needed work on his shot. As more than a 100 gathered in disbelief, Kobe launched hundreds of shots from all over the court. The session lasted until midnight, but not until Kobe had put in another 90 minutes into his greatness after a grueling game.

But that story pales in comparison to the diamond time he invested during the 2008 Olympics in Beijing. An athletic trainer named Robert published an article on Reddit recalling a moment where Kobe put in some impressive diamond time.

I've been a professional athletic trainer for about 16 years and have been able to work with a range of athletes from the high school to professional level. Right now I run in a clinic in Cincinnati and have most recently been training with some players on the Bengals.

I activated my reddit account just a moment ago and because I've been seeing the videos of Kobe's most recent dunks and the comments you guys have had to share I decided I might as well chime in what I know about the man. And let me just state by saying that this story doesn't touch on anything we don't know about Kobe but rather that he simply is not human when he is working on his craft.

I was invited to Las Vegas this past summer to help Team USA with their conditioning before they head off to London, and as we know they would eventually bring home the Gold (USA). I've had the opportunity to work with Carmelo Anthony and Dwayne Wade in the past but this would be my first interaction with Kobe. We first met three days before the first scrimmage, on the day of the first practice, early July. It was a brief conversation where we talked about conditioning, where he would like to be by the end of the summer, and we talked a little bit about the hustle of the Select Team. Then he got my number and I let him know that if he ever wanted some extra training he could hit me up any time.

The night before the first scrimmage I remember I was just watched "Casablanca" for the first time and it was about 3:30 AM. I lay in bed, slowly fading away when I hear my cell ring. It was Kobe. I nervously picked up.

"Hey, uhh Rob, I hope I'm not disturbing anything right?"

"Uhh no, what's up Kob?"

"Just wondering if you could just help me out with some conditioning work, that's all."

I checked my clock. 4:15 AM.

"Yeah sure, I'll see you in the facility in a bit."

It took me about twenty minutes to get my gear and out of the hotel. When I arrived and opened the room to the main practice floor I saw Kobe. Alone. He was drenched in sweat as if he had just taken a swim. It wasn't even 5AM.

We did some conditioning work for the next hour and fifteen minutes. Then we entered the weight room, where he would do a multitude of strength training exercises for the next 45 minutes. After that we parted ways and he went back to the practice floor to shoot. I went back to the hotel and crashed. Wow.

I was expected to be at the floor again at about 11 AM. I woke up feeling sleepy, drowsy, and almost pretty much every side effect of sleep deprivation. Thanks, Kobe. I had a bagel and headed to the practice facility.

This next part I remember very vividly. All the Team USA players were there, feeling good for the first scrimmage. LeBron was talking to Carmelo if I remember correctly and Coach Krzyzewski was trying to explain something to Kevin Durant. On the right side of the practice facility was Kobe by himself shooting jumpers. And this is how our next conversation went -- I went over to him, patted him on the back and said, "Good work this morning."

"Huh?"

"Like, the conditioning. Good work."

"Oh. Yeah, thanks Rob. I really appreciate it."

"So when did you finish?"

"Finish what?"

"Getting your shots up. What time did you leave the facility?"

"Oh just now. I wanted 800 makes so yeah, just now."

My jaw dropped. Mother of holy God. It was then that I realized that there's no surprise to why he's been as effective as he was last season. Every story about his dedication, every quote that he's said about hard work all came together and hit me like a train. It's no surprise to me now that he's dunking on players ten years younger than him and it wasn't a surprise to me earlier this year when he led the league in scoring.

Now that is not the perfect example of diamond time I don't know what is. All that work BEFORE practicing against the best competition in the world that included likes of LeBron James, Kevin Durant and Carmelo Anthony.

It comes as no surprise that when this team faced its toughest challenge in the gold medal game, it was Kobe Bryant who came to the rescue. After Spain pulled within 2 points with only 8 minutes left in the game, Team USA took a time out. That is when Kobe decided to take over the game. He scored or assisted on 11 of the next 13 points for Team USA that helped to ice the game in its most crucial moments. When you put in diamond time then you will be able to come through when it is your time to shine!

Remember that success is a journey.

Why is success a journey, because it's more about the person than the place. Success is more about you than what you do. That is why I keep saying success is yours.

You are laying the foundation vital to your future success. One of the biggest layers of that foundation is your self-confidence. Your ability to understand, believe and motivate yourself *under any circumstance* will play a repeated role in your journey of success. Notice that I did not say your journey to success. I need for you to realize that the saying is true: "Success is a journey, not a destination." For years I resisted this statement of truth and wisdom. I encourage you to avoid that same costly mistake that I made. I will help you to get started by giving you my remixed version of this quote.

DC Remix: "Success is a journey with multiple destinations."

While the wording may seem very similar the reality of the remix is that it makes a big difference. When you understand that the journey has multiple destinations that you can be excited about, it changes your perspective on the journey. When we decide to get focused on a long term destination without the glory of achieving short term goals along the way then we are setting ourselves up for disappointment and discouragement. This is one of the reasons many people quit in the middle of the journey. You cannot afford to fail when it comes to recognizing every significant step of progress that you have made along the way. It makes all the difference.

Success is about making progress toward becoming the man or woman that you were born to be. You probably have heard the saying, "Success is a journey, not a destination." That saying could not be truer. One achiever after another will tell you that the best part of their success were the moments created during the journey. They often say the arrival to the destination is anti-climactic. There is often a feeling that says, "Is this it?" You see, progress is the target, not simply acquiring material things. As a result I have a remixed version of this famous quote: "Success is a journey with multiple destinations". It is beyond important that you recognize that there are multiple destinations along your journey where you can feel proud of yourself, celebrate your achievements and recognize your progress.

Winning comes from within. Believe in yourself.
Recognize and maximize Diamond Time.
The rest will complete itself. Your greatness will inspire you to shine.

CHAPTER 6

DEVELOPING THE LION MENTATLITY

Winning is almost always linked to a peak performance. Doing your best is going to be the best way to live the life you dream about living. I encourage my daughter every day with this simple quote:

Life is best, when I'm at my best!

I tell her that the only thing I expect from her is HER best. I truly believe that conditioning ourselves to give our best is a practices that will change every area of life.

When it comes to winning, I do not know anyone who prefers the opposite. I have yet to meet a group of people who flat out say, "I actually like losing. It feels good be in last place." Losing does bother some people more than others, but in the end I do not think anyone wants to be a loser. Winning is always the goal, the question is what can we do to make sure that we are doing more winning and less losing in life.

One answer can be gained from the lion mentality. That answer is teamwork. As you may know, lions hunt and live in groups called the pride. While research why the lion is considered the king of the jungle, one recurring point was the pride. The pride is what gives the lion significant advantages over other animals in the wild.

Some researchers say that lions and tigers are 95-98% anatomically the same animal. Comparing the two ferocious big cats you will see that they are very similar. Neither of them fear another animal. They are natural predators that are not hunted by any other animal. Their biggest threats come from humans. Both are gifted hunters with a stealth ability to surprise their prey. They are both built for the hunt with retractable claws and sharp fangs to seize their prey. A tigers' roar can be heard up to 2 miles away; the lion can be heard up to 5 miles away. Both animals stand about 6 feet tall. Tigers are generally bigger, outweighing lions by 80lbs on average. They hunt similar types of animals such as deer, buffalo, antelope, zebra and wildebeests. Again, while very similar there is one big difference between two of the top predators on the planet. That difference is the pride. Tigers are solitary hunters. They exist and live their lives alone. This robs them of some advantages that the lion has. A lion is known for its courage and willingness to engage in a fight. Being in a pride gives the lion more experience fighting and hunting. It also gives the lion greater room for error. When lions hunt successfully, the entire pride gets to eat. If a tiger fails to catch its prey, they have no help to rely upon. The strength of the pride is the lion and the strength of the lion is the pride.

As you pursue success through peak performance, remember that 'teamwork makes the dream work.' Look for ways to build strong relationships with people who are hungry for greatness. Network with people who expect the best from themselves and other. Spend time surrounding yourself with gifted people because they will usually respect the gift that lies within you. Do not aim to be a lone warrior of greatness, instead focus on creating a peer group that brings out the best within you.

Be the Lion, not the Gazelle by understanding your role in different situations that you face in life.

Chapter 6 Summary Activity
How to Win: Unleashing Peak Performance

Diamond Time

❖ Unleashing peak performance requires time.

❖ What will you do to invest Diamond Time:

_____

_____

_____

❖ What will you stop doing to improve your performance?

_____

_____

_____

❖ What are some short term goals you can look forward to appreciating on your success journey?

_____

_____

_____

❖ List your DCMVP (Most Valuable Point/Principle) from this chapter.

_____

_____

❖ Why did this DCMVP stand out to you?

_____

_____

❖ How will you use this DCMVP to change your life?

_____

_____

Phase III: Possibilities
Maximizing Your Accomplishments

Possibilities are where my success becomes a reality

This phase of demanding greatness is about drawing out the best version of you. Your possibilities should inspire you to display your greatness. As you continue to pursue your possibilities with excellence and a peak performance, they begin to become realities. The growth of your vision is astronomical. The best is yet to come for you. The best of you is about to be seen for the world to admire. Pursue possibilities so big that only the best version of you can accomplish them. Once you have walked through the doors of possibility, you will realize that there are many other possibilities that exist for you.

Possibility has several definitions that caught my eye:
- one's utmost power, capacity, or ability
- a chance that something may or may not happen

This is where the monumental shifts, that have always existed, become real in your life. Again, this book was not written as a 'hype me up' for a moment type of work. It is designed to help you experience a monumental shift in your mind that will take your life in a new and upward direction. In order for this to take place in your life, you must have faith. You must believe that it is possible for you. Even with great potential and peak performance, you can reduce or eliminate your possibilities with negative beliefs. Negative beliefs about your self will contaminate your perspective and stop you from seeing what is possible. Negative beliefs about the world around you can stop you from accessing important resources that would otherwise catapult your life to new heights. Keep your mind filled with positive thoughts, positive energy and positive beliefs. Practice being positive and use possibility thinking every day.

You can access your ultimate power, capacity and ability once you become more aware of it. The incredible thing about the success formula that I am sharing with you is that it is cyclical. It keeps feeding itself as long as you keep looking for ways to improve yourself and your life.

As your performance continues to improve and give you access to higher levels of your potential, it also automatically gives you access to higher levels of possibilities as well. Possibilities exist based on the level of potential that you are accessing at a given moment in your life.

Your possibilities are actually realities waiting for you to make them happen with consistent peak performance that maximizes your God given potential. They are designed to inspire you to a level where you are dedicated to do what it takes to make them a reality.

I challenge you to pursue your possibilities. Allow your mind to explore what is possible for you. That will inspire to you consistently look for new ways to access your potential throughout your life. You will begin to notice potential that you did not even know you possessed.

Once you commit to bring your peak performance into the world new possibilities will be made available to you. This only happens when you maximize all of your abilities. You discover your limits only when you push yourself to the edge. At that point you will find that your personal growth has given you the ability to expand your limits. You will achieve more than you ever imagined.

In chapters 7-9, I will discuss key factors that impact show you how possibilities impact your life. You will learn how to recognize your opportunities, create your advantages and display your greatness. Possibilities will give you experiences that bring color and excitement to your life. They help to create memories that will be cherished forever. Your time has come to live your best life. Embrace your possibilities.

Chapter

7

My Opportunities

"The opportunity of a lifetime must be seized within the lifetime of
the opportunity."
- Leonard Havenhill, Author and Evangelist

Each of us have a unique set of opportunities available to us right
now at this moment. Opening your eyes to see what is already there
will allow you to experience life in a greater way. Your opportunities
are the gateway to your possibilities. In Phase II: Performance, we
learned about the importance to learning and preparing to become
your best. This is essential when it comes to taking advantage of
opportunities in life. The mistake you must avoid is waiting until you
see the opportunity before you get prepared for to seize the
opportunity. People who make statements like, "Once I find the job I
like then I will work on my resume" are falling behind people who
have been updating their resume before the job was made available.
Learn to live by the motto: "If you stay ready, you don't have to get
ready"

Civil rights leader Whitney Young put it like this, "It is better to be prepared for an opportunity and not have one than to have one and not be prepared."

Look at your life and recognize that right now you have opportunities available to you. Some opportunities are obvious, others are hidden. I will point out a few, but remember there are many opportunities available to your right now.

Take advantage of the opportunity to fulfill your purpose.

This opportunity will pay off for you in ways that are immeasurable. Once you begin to live life on purpose you will find that you get paid in your soul before you get paid in your bank account.

Last summer I was invited to speak to a group of students heading to college. I accepted the invitation because of the strong relationship I have with the coordinator of this pre-college program. Due to the pressing needs of a few projects that I need to complete, I did not have a lot of time to spare for this invitation. In addition, budget complications prevented the program from being able to compensate me for my services. Based on these factors, I made up my mind that I would speak for 15-20 minutes. My goal was to inspire these young leaders to create a future so bright that they would need to put on sunglasses to look at it. What happened next was surprise that no one was expecting.

Once I entered the room, the energy was electric. These young students were ready for greatness. As I started my speech, I quickly diverted from the notes that would have led me to speak for 15-20 minutes. I entered what I call 'the flow'. This is where I am so engulfed in the moment that the words of my speech flow through me into the audience. That night the flow was strong, so strong in fact that I lost track of time. After my conclusion, we opened up the mic for questions. One question after the next continued to come. One young lady came to tears as she shared how my words touched her heart and gave her the courage to believe that she could be successful at the college level. Just when it appeared that we were done, another student raised her hand and said, "I don't have a question. I just want you to stay and keep talking. Your words are inspiring to me." As she said that, I became curious about how long I had been with this ambitious group. Her statement would make perfect sense if I had stuck to my 15-20 minute time frame, which I know I did not. When I looked at my watch, I saw that we had spent nearly 3 hours together! Looking back, I am not sure what was more amazing, the 3 hours or the fact that when I left they were still wanting more. One thing is certain. Purpose paid me, even though I was not sure that the program would. I left that room feeling fulfilled. I knew that I had given my gift in a way that changed lives. In addition to that, the program worked out their budgetary issues and sent me a check in the mail. I told you, living life on purpose will pay you in your soul before you get paid in your bank account.

The greatest compensation of purpose is not the money you earn from it, but the fulfillment you gain because of it.

Look for the opportunity to inspire someone to live their dreams.

Every week, I take a team of college students with me to volunteer our time at the local Boys and Girls in Lansing. This is one of our ways to give back through our time. Every week, we are inspiring today's youth to create tomorrow's future. It has become so popular that my volunteers are recruiting their friends to come with us.

The teens at the Boys and Girls club have begun to look forward to our visits. Initially, they were acting 'too cool for school' as we used to say. Now we can tell that they are listening. They are beginning to value the messages and information that we are passing along to them. They are realizing that they can take steps today what will allow them to live the life of their dreams.

We embrace the opportunity to inspire.

You will always have the opportunity to make the adjustment.

Currently, I am divorced and co-parenting my 6 year old daughter with her mom. This was not my plan for life at all, but in life it is about making the adjustment. Life will throw many things your way unexpectedly. One day, after the divorce, she asked if this was the best thing for Savannah. I told her flatly that we have to shift our focus from the best thing to the next best thing. When the best thing is no longer available, we should not waste too much time moping over what was lost. Grieving has its place in life, but it must also have an expiration date. If you do not give your grief a deadline then it will sap you of the energy needed to move forward with your life.

I tell my students the same thing. If a 4.0 is no longer mathematically possible in a certain class, then put all your focus on the 3.5 because it is the next best thing under the circumstances. Too many of us ruin tomorrow by spending today's energy focusing on what happened yesterday.

Taking my own advice, I've decided that I am going to become a "Co-Parenting All Star" with my sights set on go down in the Co-Parenting Hall of Fame. This is something that I created in my own mind to adjust my parental expectations. With this new goal, my focus is different. It is easier to co-parent without unnecessary distractions. Her mom has since re-married. I view raising my daughter as a team effort; my ex-wife and her husband are both my teammates. Our goal is to find the best way to raise Savannah and meet her needs.

This was not an easy decision for me. It took time for me to develop the maturity required to accept the next best thing. I had to refuse to allow selfishness guide my decisions. I had to fight my pride regarding another man being involved in my daughter's life.

About two years ago, she started calling him daddy. This raised my eyebrows immediately. Quickly, I had to compose myself because I was ready to snap. Thoughts flooded my mind.

"I'm your only daddy."
"Never call another man daddy around me."
"Don't forget who your ready daddy is."

These thoughts immediately made me revert back to my childhood. I remembered the tension between my mother and grandma. I also remembered how it made me feel to be in the middle of the turmoil. Since I lived with my grandma until age 8, I would call her mama like everybody else did. This infuriated my mom. In my mind I would try to switch up the times when I called my grandma, mama. I was trying not to anger my mother, but also trying to stay true to how I felt about my grandma. The turmoil that created in my young mind was draining.

Remembering my own experiences forced me to respond logically, not with my emotions. I decided to ask my daughter some questions. I found out that she asked him if she could start calling him daddy. She felt like he cared for and loved her. She was looking for a way to express that emotion. She was excited about the idea of having two daddies. When I asked her why, her answer stuck with me. "I've never had two dads before", she said with her cute little voice. "I think it's cool to have two dads." She went on to say that she knew I was her real dad, but he felt like her dad too. I took a moment to rationalize things and came to this conclusion. What little girl would not want the feeling of having a dad around every day in her life? My parenting time is 10 days a month, but it made sense to me that she would want to feel like she had a fatherly presence in her life every day of the month. Considering the circumstances, I can only provide that during my time with her. I realized that she was seeking something that she deserved.

I had to grow to a point where every decision truly has to be about her best interest, not massaging my ego and emotions. Also, I am not pretending that everything is smooth sailing. There have been multiple occasions where the waters were rough, but that comes with the territory. Making the adjustment in life will not be easy, but it will be necessary.

One of the most overlooked opportunities is the opportunity to correct a mistake:
An old error can lead to new era

New horizons lie just beyond the lessons you learn from your last mistake. The wisdom you have gained allows you to handle mistakes differently that you did during your survival phase. During that phase you were focused on surviving your mistakes, but now you are capable of maximizing your mistakes.

When you have the level of confidence that allows you to make mistakes without feeling insecure you are ready to unleash another level of brilliance into the ear. You have official gone form a mistake maker to a mistake maximizer. This is what happened years ago at 3M when one of their most successful products as created by mistake.

There were actually two accidents that lead to the invention of the Post-It note. The first was by Spencer Silver. According to the former Vice President of Technical Operations for 3M Geoff Nicholson (now retired), in 1968, Silver was working at 3M trying to create super strong adhesives for use in the aerospace industry in building planes. Instead of a super strong adhesive, though, he accidentally managed to create an incredibly weak, pressure sensitive adhesive agent called Acrylate Copolymer Microspheres.

This adhesive did not interest 3M management as it was seen as too weak to be useful. It did have two interesting features, though. The first is that, when stuck to a surface, it can be peeled away without leaving any residue. Specifically, the acrylic spheres only stick well to surfaces where they are tangent to the surface, thus allowing weak enough adhesion to be able to be peeled easily. The second big feature is that the adhesive is re-usable, thanks to the fact that the spheres are incredibly strong and resist breaking, dissolving, or melting. Despite these two notable features, no one, not even Silver himself, could think up a good marketable use for it. Thus, even with Silver promoting it for five years straight to various 3M employees, the adhesive was more or less shelved.

Finally, in 1973, when Geoff Nicholson was made products laboratory manager at 3M, Silver approached him immediately with the adhesive and gave him samples to play with. Silver also suggested what he saw as his best idea for what to use the adhesive for, making a bulletin board with the adhesive sprayed on it. One could then stick pieces of paper to the bulletin board without tacks, tape, or the like. The paper could subsequently be easily removed without any residue being left on the sheets. While this was a decent idea, it wasn't seen as potentially profitable enough as annual bulletin board sales are fairly low.

Now enter the second accident by chemical engineer Art Fry. Besides working at 3M as a Product Development Engineer and being familiar with Silver's adhesive thanks to attending one of Silver's seminars on the low-tack adhesive, he also sung in a church choir in St. Paul, Minnesota. One little problem he continually had to deal with was accidentally losing his song page markers in his hymn book while singing, with them falling out of the hymnal. From this, he eventually had the stroke of genius to use some of Silver's adhesive to help keep the slips of paper in the hymnal. Fry then suggested to Nicholson and Silver that they were using the adhesive backwards. Instead of sticking the adhesive to the bulletin board, they should "put it on a piece of paper and then we can stick it to anything."

This initially proved easier said than done, in terms of practical application. It was easy enough to get the adhesive on the paper, but the early prototypes had the problem that the adhesive would often detach from the paper and stay on the object the paper was stuck to, or, at least, leave some of the adhesive behind in this way. There was no such problem with the bulletin boards Silver had made because he had specifically made them so that the adhesive would bond better with the board than the paper. Two other 3M employees now entered the scene, Roger Merrill and Henry Courtney. The two were tasked with coming up with a coating that could be put on the paper to make the adhesive stay bonded to it and not be left behind on whatever the paper was stuck to when it was removed, a task at which they were ultimately successful at achieving.

Interestingly, because management at 3M still didn't think the product would be commercially successful, they more or less shelved it for three years, even though the Post-It notes were extremely popular internally at 3M labs during that span. Finally, in 1977, 3M began running test sale runs of the Post-It note, then called "Press 'n Peel", in a certain areas in four different cities to see if people would buy and use the product. It turned out, no one much did, which confirmed in the minds of the executives that it wasn't a good commercial product.

Luckily for offices the world over, Nicholson and Joe Ramey, Nicholson's boss, didn't feel like giving up yet. They felt the marketing department had dropped the ball in that they hadn't given businesses and people samples of the product to use to let them see for themselves how useful the notes could be. So a year after the initial flop, 3M tried again to introduce the Post-It note to the world, this time giving huge amounts of free sample Post-It note pads away in Boise, Idaho, with the campaign deemed "The Boise Blitz". This time, the re-order rate went from almost nothing, in the previous attempt, to 90% of the people and businesses that had received the free samples. For reference, this was double the best initial rate 3M had ever seen for any other product they'd introduced. Two years later, the Post-It note was released throughout the United States.

So after 5 years of constant rejection for the adhesive and another seven years in development and initial rejection, Post-It notes were finally a hit and have since become a mainstay in offices the world over, today being one of the top five bestselling office supply products in the world.

There is a genius and brilliance to mastering the ability to use your error to start an era. The Post It Notes era at 3M all started from an error. The same thing happens when you and I look for ways to grow from our mistakes. When you succeed you have an opportunity to EARN; when you fail and take the L properly you can L-EARN.

The opportunity to make history by making a monumental shift in your life.

This is not about motivation for a moment. This is about creating a monumental shift in a new direction for your life. I define a monumental shift as:

"A significant and exceptionally great change inside of you by which you can mark the moment you when exchanged who you were and what you had for who you were created to be and what was meant to be yours. This shift will allow you to now flow into a new fresh path that is existing in your life for the first time; thereby giving you the opportunity to experience life in a way that you have never explored before."

As you read this part of the book I want you to know that you are in rare territory. Research says that most people never buy or read a book for the rest of their lives after leaving high school. Those who do buy books, often do not ever read the book. Looking at those people who both buy and start to read the book, on average they only read approximately 12% of the book. You are different. Your voracious hunger and desire to become the best version of yourself has led you here.

There is a newness is available to you right now as an opportunity to enter an open door to a higher dimension of your future. Accept the statement above as truth for you and your monumental shift will become real in your life.

When you consider the importance of this shift, it makes the existence of the opposite even more dangerous to your future. You can never afford to be shiftless. The lack of ambition, aspiration or otherwise lacking incentive is unacceptable for you.

Your opportunity to experience a monumental shift creates an advantage that makes you unstoppable force on your path of greatness.

CHAPTER 7

DEVELOPING THE LION MENTATLITY

Every day is full of opportunity when you possess the lion mentality. Through the eyes of the lion opportunity is defined by legacy.

The lion has a great reputation. It is known as king of the jungle. The respect they attract is unlike most any other in the animal kingdom. However, that does not mean that the lion's path is without adversity. Tough times will visit us all.

Having the lion's mentality does not mean that every day will be perfect and filled with happiness. There will be dark days, tough times and challenging moments. Just as lions are sometimes injured during the hunt, you can be scarred by some of the battles you face in your life. I read a quote that makes my point perfectly. "Never be ashamed of a scar. It simply means you were stronger than whatever tried to hurt you."

I like to take it one step further and say it is time to make adversity work for you and create a legacy scar. When you already have the scar, you must choose to give it meaning. A legacy scar is a symbol that life has given you a negative experience that you turned into a success story. Legacy scars can teach new lessons and give growth that you could not have received any other way.

Always remember that your hunger does not go away simply because life is taking you through tough times. Wounded lions still have to hunt. Wounds do not take away your greatness; but they do test your greatness. There are times where you will need to push through the pain to reach your goals. These moments will reveal to you a level of strength that you did not even realize you had.

Lastly, it is important to know that a strong identity will lead you to great opportunity. It will guide your actions and help you to do the right thing at the right time. Too often I have seen people try to 'prove themselves' by doing things without proper timing. In the name of 'keeping it real' some people squander opportunities. For example, if you are interviewing for a job in a professional environment that is not the time to make a personal statement by wearing a jogging suit and sneakers. Some may say, "But I don't want to be fake". I respond by saying that you are being real....real true to your dreams. There are times in life where you must adapt to the situation based on the goals you are looking to achieve in that moment.

Notice that a lion is known for its roar, but more importantly the lion knows when to roar. Lions do not roar during the hunt. Why not you may ask, because that would alert their prey and destroy the purpose of the hunt itself. Lions do not roar to show off their ability, they roar with purpose. They do not worry about being labeled a fake lion. They do not take the mentality that 'I will roar whenever I want to.' They wisely understand their purpose in the moment. Once the successful hunt is complete, the lion will roar loudly to tell every animal that notices the scent of fresh meat in the air not to come too close. At that time they are roaring with purpose, not simply to 'keep it real.'

Be the Lion, not the Gazelle by learning to value each opportunity for success.

Chapter 7 Summary Activity
My Opportunities

❖ What opportunities are available to you presently?

_____

_____

❖ Name three reasons why each opportunity will inspire you to maximize your potential by unleashing your elite performance.

1. _____

2. _____

3. _____

❖ List your DCMVP (Most Valuable Point/Principle) from this chapter.

_____

_____

❖ Why did this DCMVP stand out to you?

_____

_____

❖ How will you use this DCMVP to change your life?

_____

_____

Chapter

8

My Advantage

"I grew up with every disadvantage needed for success."
-Larry Ellison, CEO, Oracle

The combination of skills, talents, abilities and work ethic you have invested into your life have created specific advantages for you. Becoming aware of these advantages will be the best and fastest way for you to maximize them. Once you use your advantages to your advantage then you will experience a change in your vantage point in life.

**Give the advantage to your children with good parenting.
They will see what you say!**

As parents we have the power to speak, life or death, over our children. What we say to them and about them will manifest within and around them. It is that manifestation that society sees when they look at your child. The words of YOUR mouth are laying and setting the foundation for how people will receive, encounter and interact with your child.

I have been saying, for years now, that my daughter Savannah is "full of life", any time that someone asks me about her or how she is doing. It is my mantra regarding my princess. She is and always will be full of life. It is a contributing factor to why she is open to receive more of what life has to offer her.

I saw the fruits of my labors and belief play out right before my eyes. This past summer during a visit to the beach we crossed paths with another family and causally engaged in a conversation. Then an older lady stopped as if something arrested her attention and said, "Ah, she's so full of life." It is no coincidence that a woman who has never met Savannah would say that about her. That was AWESOME! I am so thankful that Savannah is "so full of life." And I want to say thank you to the kind lady for the upgraded remix to my statement....not just "full of life", but "so full of life!"

Too many parents speak and release unwanted, negative and stifling words over their children.

"He's so bad."
"She's so stubborn and hard headed!"
"He just won't listen to nobody!"
"She is gonna get herself into trouble with that little attitude of hers."

WE MUST STOP! We are killing off the life potential of our children with each negative syllable that we are releasing over OUR OWN children. This practiced habit must be upgraded immediately. I call forth a change....a monumental shift in a new direction for parents and their children...starting now!

The advantage of having a winning attitude.

Have you ever wondered how two people can come from the same background, school, neighborhood or household and completely different outcomes in life? This question has always been one that held my attention. How is it that some people seem to display great skill or technique in handling life's toughest situations? They seem to make it easy to live out that saying, "what doesn't kill me will make me stronger." What is their secret? What do they know that I do not?

I have come to find out that these people usually have a greater understanding of what the pain represents in their life. They have mastered the ability to define the meaning of the pain and find ways to use it to their advantage. The following story shows a clear example of this:

Two brothers sat at a cluttered kitchen table. The house reeked of stale alcohol and trash. Flies hovered over piles of dirty dishes. Dad was drunk on the couch. One child was parked in front of the TV while the other was focused in his homework. One father, two boys. One situation, an alcoholic father and an absent mother. Both boys experienced the same hell on earth living with verbal and physical abuse and neglect every day.

One brother ran with a fast crowd who helped him find an escape. Like his father, he found it in drugs and alcohol. This second-generation alcoholic lived from bottle to bottle, barely finding odd jobs, earning just enough money to continue his habit. The second brother buried himself in his schoolwork. A teacher praised his efforts, and consequently he excelled. He worked hard and won a scholarship to an Ivy League school. He went on to become a well-respected lawyer. One day a newspaper chose to write a front page story on their local hero. The reporter asked the young man, "Is it true your father was an alcoholic?"

"It's true. I had an alcoholic father. I decided early on I wasn't going to waste my life the way he did. That's why I am where I am today."

Meanwhile the first brother continued on his path of destruction. Eventually his employer gave him the choice of losing his job or entering a rehab clinic. He chose the clinic. The counselor in the rehab program listened as he described his childhood: "I had an alcoholic father, that's why I am where I am today." Same home. Same father. But different outcomes.

We cannot choose the events to begin our lives, but we can choose to control the outcomes of our lives.

I challenge you to take this philosophy as your own. Embrace it and you will be empowered by it. Your pain is meant to develop you, not destroy you. Write it down, memorize it, put it on your wall and tattoo it on your heart. Commit yourself right now to use EVERY painful situation to your advantage. No matter what it is, you can find a way to make it serve you. There are times where this will be easier said than done, do it anyway. There will be times where it may take a long than expected before it works in your favor, see it through. The key is to stay focused, but not on how the pain makes you feel. Instead focus on how the opportunity to master your pain is the greatest skill you may ever learn in life.

Life will never stop throwing punches your way. The good news is that you can get stronger with every blow. You must strengthen your mind and spirit by getting stronger on a daily basis.

I heard Les Brown say "You're either in a problem, just left one or headed toward one." Face that fact. Deal with your reality, but do not miss the point. The point of pain is to help you find your purpose.

Possibility Thinking will give you a spiritual, mental and emotional advantage.

My suggestion to you is simple. Invest 15 minutes every day thinking about nothing but positive possibilities. This will recondition the way you look at yourself as well as your opportunities. It will give you a mental advantage in life. The best time to practice possibility thinking is in the morning before you start your day. It will allow you to start the day off with a clean slate, before the day's activities try to distract you. If you find it too challenging to do all 15 minutes at one time then you can break it up. You might find it easier to do 5 minutes, 3 times a day. The key is to make sure you get this time into your day consistently. It is a small amount of time that will make a big difference in your thinking. It's only 10% of the 1440 minutes you have each day. Dwelling in possibility thinking will help to protect you from the all the negativity that exists in the outside world. Inner strength will always overcome outward obstacles as long as you consistently replenish your inner strength.

Greatness is seeking to use every advantage to their advantage; mediocrity is looking to prove irrelevant points that provide invisible rewards.

CHAPTER 8

DEVELOPING THE LION MENTATLITY

During a lunch meeting one day while talking to a friend about his trip the African safari, I learned about the lion mentality in a way that fascinated me. He spoke to me about the impact that the lion's presence had on every person and every animal that around it. As the tour guide described the scene, everybody's eyes were fixated on the lion. Every animal did the same; even the chimpanzees in the trees kept a constant awareness of the location of the lion. It is almost as if the lion's every move dictated the moves of everyone and everything around it. Meanwhile, the lion was not paying specific attention to any of the other animals. It was causally walking at its own pace. Enjoying the moment as it had decided it would. As he described the scene it was obvious to me that the lion had established an extreme comfort in knowing its role within the environment that it was living in.

The lion's mentality is a mentality that creates a sense of control and expectations. We must adopt the type of mentality that allows us to feel in control and expect success in all situations. This will give you the freedom to dream at new levels and achieve more than rapidly than ever before. It will inspire confidence and create a greater sense of fulfillment.

One time I had someone say, well isn't it easy for a lion to be confident when it is the king of the jungle. I had to remind them that it is not due to the lion having every advantage working in its favor. Think about this: who is faster between the lion and the gazelle? Many will quickly say the lion because we remember the times where we've seen the lion catch the gazelle. But remember what I mentioned earlier. The lion only catches the gazelle 3 times out of 10 tries. And during the 3 successful attempts, the lion has to be stealth just to get close enough to start its chase of the gazelle. This is because the gazelle is faster than the lion. The speed advantage is in the favor of the gazelle, but the lion's mentality uses strategy to overcome their disadvantages.

When the lion hunts other animals the principle is the same even though the strategy is not. Lions are faster than buffalo. There is no need to worry about losing a foot race that hunt. However there is another challenge: size. The lion is not bigger than the buffalo. The size advantage is in the favor of the buffalo; again, the lion's mentality uses strategy to overcome their disadvantages. When lions hunt buffalo they use the strength of their numbers to overwhelm the massive animal. There are usually three or more lions attacking one buffalo from multiple angles. The lion mentality does not change the goal, but when necessary it will change the strategy to re-gain the advantage.

The lion mentality equips and empowers you to look at your 'disadvantages' with a different attitude. The lion mentality says my strategy gives me the advantage over my enemy. Strategy is key!

Be the Lion, not the Gazelle by creating an advantage even when it seems like you are at a disadvantage.

Chapter 8 Summary Activity
My Advantages

❖ What advantages have you created through your performance?

_____

_____

❖ Name two advantages you can create with elite performance

1. _____

2. _____

❖ List your DCMVP (Most Valuable Point/Principle) from this chapter.

_____

_____

❖ Why did this DCMVP stand out to you?

_____

_____

❖ How will you use this DCMVP to change your life?

_____

_____

Chapter
9

My Greatness

"We all die. The goal isn't to live forever; the goal is to create
something that will."
-Chuck Palahniuk

The culmination of all that you are and all that you are meant to be
can be summed up in one word: Greatness. It is a word that grabs the
attention of everyone. Greatness is magnetic, inspirational, and
contagious. Learn how to 'put it all together' so that you can
'Demand Greatness' on a daily basis.

Going beyond success means that you have you sights set on
greatness. You are looking beyond the things you gain from success
and have decided to focus on the character you gain from greatness.
This is where you will find the greatest challenges of your life
because they are divinely positioned to make sure you are qualified
to unleash the greatest potential in your life. You will need three
things to maximize your qualification for greatness:

Great Beliefs:
Feed yourself great information

Greatness is a mentality that separates itself from mediocre thinkers. This pattern of thoughts leads us to talk differently than other people who accept mediocrity. We become language detectives; constantly searching to purify our words by deleting doubt and building belief. Our beliefs are build primary upon our words and thoughts. The combination of those two things impacts the way we feel, which in turn affects the decisions we make. Once we have made decisions then actions are guaranteed to follow, which leads us to form habits. Those habits are so strong that they form our character and lead us to our destiny in life.

Using this way of thinking you can look at where you are today and trace a path backwards to see how you got there. If you do not like where you are (your destiny/destination) then take a look at how your character has lead you there. Next you can ask yourself which habits created the character that I possess. Then you can evaluate the actions that instilled those habits into your life. As you do that you will find the decisions you made before taking those actions. Every decision has a root in an emotion that you had at the time of the decision. Finally you can identify what made you feel that way by looking at the words and thoughts that started this entire process in your life.

This poem illustrates the point perfectly:

Watch your words, they become thoughts.
Watch your thoughts, they become emotions.
Watch your emotions, they become decisions.
Watch your decisions, they become actions.
Watch your actions, they become habits.
Watch your habits, they become character.
Watch your character, for it becomes destiny.

Here is an example of one of my core beliefs that have stood the test of time and adversity:

If you can see it, you can solve it.

That is what I tell myself now whenever I am faced with a problem that feels overwhelming. Whether you believe the Bible or not, you cannot refute its long lasting status as a text that is rich with truth and useful instructions for living a high quality life. In one passage it says, "He will never give you more that you can bear...but with every challenge he will make a way of escape". I believe that if the problem in on your path then the solution to that same problem is not very far away. That solution is in you, around you or within someone close to you.

The following analogy has helped me throughout life and I am sure it will help you too. See yourself like that math textbook from grade school. In the teacher's edition there is a section toward the back of the book that has answers to questions listed in chapters throughout the book. Not only do those chapters include examples of how to solve the problems, they also have the actual answer to the questions in the back of the book! Life is a lot like that. Problems are presented, examples are given and answers are within reach. The key is to never forget this simple fact.

I have faced many problems during my life and I can assure that I signed up for none of them. I did not submit any applications to receive the challenges that were on my path. Regardless, I had to quickly adapt to the situations that were created as a result of life's challenges. I often asked and said: "Why does life keep throwing me negative situations?" "Why do bad things keep happening to me?", "It's not fair!", "How come, nobody else is going through what I'm going through?"

It wasn't until I went to college that I discovered the wise words of Charles Swindoll:

"The longer I live, the more I realize the impact of attitude on life.
Attitude, to me, is more important than facts.
It is more important than the past, than education, than money, than circumstances,

Than failures, than successes, than what other people think or say or do.
It is more important than appearance, giftedness or skill.
It will make or break a company...a church....a home.
The remarkable thing is we have a choice every day regarding the attitude we will embrace for that day.
We cannot change our past...we cannot change the fact that people will act in a certain way. We cannot change the inevitable.
The only thing we can do is play on the one string we have, and that is our attitude...*I am convinced that life is 10% what happens to me and 90% how I react to it.*
And so it is with you...we are in charge of our attitudes."

My take away from this quote can be described in the formula listed below:

Event + Response = Outcome

I will never forget all the light bulbs that went off in my head when I read that statement. It became clear to me that day that WHAT happened to me can NEVER be the complete story. According to this formula my response is required to create an outcome. That told me that I am never out of the equation for anything that happens in my life. I always have a degree of impact, a percentage of control, and a final say. Remember that the response occurs after the event. The event never has the last word on the outcome of my life. The last word is left up to my response, which is my choice.

I have to consistently remind myself during tough times that I am unstoppable and the best is yet to come. These are also core beliefs. They help to program my mind to find a way to victory. They help me to never accept defeat. When that negative voice in my mind says, "Life is not fair" I responded by saying, "yeah, but it's not final either." These beliefs allow me to respond with optimism and faith.

Great Habits

Our habits lay the groundwork for the rest of our lives. My favorite quote about habits comes from Samuel Johnson. "The chains of habit are too weak to be felt until they are too strong to be broken." This truth can work for us negatively or positively. Bad habits can cripple you from reaching your potential while great habits can equip you to become unstoppable in unleashing your greatness into the world.

Habit 1: Be committed to take the next action. Regardless of the result, you must be ready to take the next action step in your journey. The key is to make it a habit to evaluate yourself. This is necessary to prepare you to adjust your actions as you move forward.

Habit 2: Moving forward. Where focus goes, energy flows. Make it a habit in life to look forward, but only glace backward. Distractions are the number one factor is your failings. Eliminate them by focusing on what ahead of you. Dwelling in the past only serves to bring more of your past into your future. If you did not like it then, you will not like it in the future either. Stop dragging bad things from your past into a future. Your future is a blank canvas that can be used to create the most beautiful picture ever. Using negative past experiences is like taking old crusty paint brush and dried up paint to create your new picture. It will not work. Your skill will be compromised by those inadequate tools. The same is true in life. If you want new results, then you have to use new tools. Your future can everything you dreamed. Commit to looking forward and refuse to allow your past to contaminate the bright future ahead of you.

Habit 3: Talk yourself into greatness. The conversations you have with yourself contain the most important words in your life. You are capable of convincing yourself of anything you want to believe, so why not convince yourself of your greatness! Muhammad Ali is famous for his brass trash talking. He intimidated and frustrated opponents with his catchy sayings and quick wit. But the most important thing he did was convince himself of his own greatness. He did not wait for others to validate him. He validated himself with quotes like, "I am the greatest. I said that even before I knew I was. I figured that if I said it enough, I would convince the world that I really was the greatest." Ali realized how powerful his words were for his life; he knew he could control his belief by controlling the words that came out of his mouth.

"It's the repetition of affirmations that leads to belief. And once that belief becomes a deep conviction, things begin to happen."
–Muhammad Ali

Ali knew that the great habit of talking himself into greatness would breathe life into the great belief he held in his heart. If it worked for Muhammad Ali then it can work for you!

It will not be easy though. I remember one time when I was looking at all of my bills, late fees and garnishments. It was depressing. Then I imagined a blind man asking me if I could see my garnishments and fees. As I nodded my head yes, this imaginary blind man said, "that means you can also see ways to make enough money to solve the problem." When my car broke down in the middle of winter I imagined a man in a wheelchair asking me if I could walk to the bus stop. Again nodding yes, this imaginary man in a wheelchair said, "Then you can also walk toward a brighter future" The point is clear. You can talk yourself into greatness, but you must make it a habit.

Great People

I offer this advice to you because I have first taken it for myself. As you have read, in my journey many predecessors have paved the way ahead of me and pulled me toward greater levels of personal growth, skill development and life success.

There are three types of people you must have if you want to have a life of sustained greatness. You need people who pull you, people who pace you and people who push you.

People who pull you are your predecessors. They are ahead of you on the road to success. You can learn from them easily because they stretch you. As they share their experiences with you, always be open to their wisdom. It will open doors and shorten your learning curve in ways that will astonish you. Even when they are not speaking to you directly, it's like their actions are saying, you can do more with your life. They inspire you by what they have done.

I have felt the pull from many people in my life. Joshua Gillespie has played this role in my life from the day I met him. He's like a big brother leading the way. I met Josh during my freshman year at MSU. He took me under his wing and showed me many life lessons that still remain with me today. I also feel the pull from people who are famous and successful. When I look at Tony Robbins, Kobe Bryant, Will Smith, Kevin Hart and Gary Vaynerchuk I feel the inspirational pull to be more in my own life. I fully believe that one day I will work on projects with one or more of them. I already have an ideas waiting for the day we cross paths. Call me a dreamer and I will call you right. That's what the pull does, it causes you to dream BIG.

People who pace you are your peers. They are alongside of you on the road to success. You share common experiences with them in real time. This builds a special connection that allows them to inspire you in a different way that your predecessors. They inspire you by what they are doing.

I have friends like Shannon Cason (accomplished storyteller), M Reese Everson (attorney and author), Tanya Upthegrove (MBA, activist) who fit this category for me. Honestly, I have so many friend to mention that pace me. These people come to mind because they have played a specific role in my speaking career.

People who push you are your pupils. They are behind you on the road to success. They are amazed by you. In their eyes you are the predecessor. You benefit from their energy, excitement and anticipation for your continued progress. They inspire you by their expectations of what they think you are going to do next.

Al Martin comes to mind first when I think about people who push me. This young brother is a sports broadcaster, already has his own radio and TV show to go along with an Emmy! Remember the name because you will see him on ESPN one day. Also, there are a few hungry 'lions' on my team right now that provide a push. I look forward to seeing how they develop under my leadership. Lastly, a group that pushed me in a way that I will never forget is the original group of student leaders in a retention program at Michigan State

Univeristy called, The Advantage. They are 23 of the most special people that I have ever worked with. I'm tempted to list them all by name, but they know who they are. They left a legacy at MSU that is still standing today. Together, under the leadership of Eric Thomas, we said that we were going to make history by changing the culture forever...and we did!

Greatness requires the personal push.

There will be moments when you will know exactly what to do; knowledge is not the problem. You understand how to get it done; instruction is not what you are lacking. The problem will be that you do not feel like doing it. You may even have legit reasons why. It could be physical or mental pain. You might have fears rooted in past failures. Your comfort zone might be the reason. Or you could simple be tired from all of the battles in your life. Whatever your reason may be this is where I challenge you to do as the greats do. The greats do it anyway. They find way to push themselves beyond the limits that ordinary people decide live by.

The greats realize that purpose is always greater than pleasure. They know that what feels good to you may not always be good for you. They operate knowing that one year from now, they will be glad that they got started today. In moments of challenge they are aware that decisions dictate destiny.

You will have great results or great regrets; the choice is yours.

The same greatness that is in them is also within you. You know it is. You feel it when you allow yourself to dream. It is the voice in your head that whispers, "You can do it." I am here to remind you that no one can give you the personal push. Just as the lion is inspired from within, you must become self-motivated in a way that empowers you to take aggressive action on your dreams.

Success Is Yours
Now is the time to unleash!

When an animal is on a leash, the leash is designed to limit how far it can go from the opposite end of the leash. Anything within the reach of the leash can still come in contact with the full power of the animal. However, anything beyond the reach of that leash is safe from the dog because the leash is restraining its ability to go beyond a certain point. Well your potential for greatness has been on a leash. Are there dreams that are beyond your reach? What goals are beyond your grasp? Think about the ambitions that you cannot achieve because you have been limiting yourself. Your unleashing happens the moment you break free from past doubts, thoughts and people that held you back.

"To each there comes in their lifetime a special moment when they are figuratively tapped on the shoulder and offered the chance to do a very special thing, unique to theme and fitted to their talents. What a tragedy if that moment finds them unprepared or unqualified for that which could have been their finest hour. "
–Sir Winston Churchill

My goal during this entire book has been to share my story in a way that inspires you to come in touch with your inner greatness. I am convinced that you will never go back to being who you used to be once you have one good taste of being who you were born to be. Coming in contact with your true greatness gives an instant addiction to that feeling of fulfillment. Nothing can compare.

Success Is Yours
Now is the time to get right!

A certain pastor was having trouble preparing his sermon on Saturday morning. He was in his study, thinking, reflecting and trying to draft out things. No ideas were coming. He desperately needed to put together the sermon for the following day. His wife had to go to buy groceries and his 5 year old son was playing by himself, making loud playful noises in the sitting room.

Slightly irritated and fully distracted, the pastor went to the sitting room to get his son to calm down. "Johnny," he said, "you are disturbing daddy. I need to prepare a sermon for tomorrow"

Johnny replied, "Daddy, do you know that an airplane's wings are very, very long?" He was gleeful and playful. Suddenly, the pastor had an idea. He went to his study, brought back an old magazine, tore out the central page that had the map of the world and ripped it into several pieces. Then he said to Johnny, "You know what? If you put together this picture, I will give you $5". He assumed that it would keep Johnny quiet and be busy for a very long time, giving him room to prepare his sermon.

However, in less than 5 minutes Johnny was back in his study. "Daddy, I am done. Come and see it." His father went with him to the sitting room to see. Indeed, the pieces had been put together.

"How did you do it so fast, Johnny?" the pastor asked.

"Well, daddy, I noticed that there was the picture of a man behind the map. So I thought it would be easier to put the picture of man together. When I did, I flipped it over and the map was all put together too."

Instantly a flood of inspiration filled the pastor's soul. Now he knew what his message would be: If the man is right, the world will be right!

Too often in life, we try to fix our world when we should be focused on fixing ourselves. Once we are right, our world will be right. Our world is only a reflection of us. This entire book has been a guide to getting yourself right so you can unleash your power. Frederick Douglass once said that power yields nothing unless there is a demand. Now is your time. Today is your day. Demand your power by demanding greatness.

Your best life is waiting for you to step up and take hold of it. The greatest version of yourself is only one decision away.

Make the decision to demand greatness because success is already yours!

Through the Eyes of the Lion

CHAPTER 9

DEVELOPING THE LION MENTATLITY

Greatness is found within, but it will have its greatest impact when you understand the world around you. The lion mentality understands that today matters, but so does tomorrow. That is why legacy is important.

When a lion and gazelle meet in the wild there is only one thing that happens next…it's off to the races! The gazelle is thinking "this is not a dress rehearsal, it's the real deal!" There is no time for second guessing. I'm sure they do not stop to say, "Is that really a lion?"

They run now and figure the rest out later. It is every gazelle for themselves. I've even seen footage where the instinct to stop and help kicked in for one gazelle. The gazelle stop and turned as a fellow gazelle slipped to the ground. In that brief moment it was as if the gazelle was going to help, but that thought was quickly interrupted by the ferocious lion heading toward them full speed. At that point, I assume the wannabe helpful gazelle said, "Whelp, I tried; but I gotta go!" Obviously, I'm adding a comical tone to the story with my imagination, but the core of the story is the same. The gazelle understands that it has zero margin for error when the lion shows up. They cannot afford to lose that race, not even once. If they do then it's 'game over'.

The gazelle's reward for winning the race is different that the lion's reward. When the gazelle beats a lion today its reward is what? You guessed it, they get to live life a little longer. The next time they are hunted by the lion and escape what is their reward for that effort? If you said they get to live life a little longer, then again you were right. Do you see a pattern? The gazelle must put in maximum effort, with little room for error, and their reward is the same in each instance. They simple get to live a little longer. They are not upgrading their lives by winning the race with the lion. The gazelle mentality in life does not allow you to accumulate rewards. It is simply about survival to see another day. Their primary reward is the escape. It's like the many people who live check to check. They work hard, feel overwhelmed by their expenses and in too many cases their reward is the ability to pay their bills and barely make it by. The moral is sadly the same; they are like the gazelle. Their life is built around being in a position where there is little room for mistakes, but big consequences to pay when mistakes happen. There is a better way to approach life, it's called the lions' mentality.

The lion's reward is much different and much better. The goal for the lion is not escape, but elevation. This is the mentality we must embrace as we demand greatness on a daily basis in our lives. Demand greatness by looking for ways to upgrade and elevate everything around you. Refuse to be intimidate by challenges. Seek to solve problems with a positive attitude. Commit to becoming the best version of yourself. This the lion's mentality. It's about legacy, not survival. The impossible becomes possible when you demand greatness.

Be the Lion, not the Gazelle by focusing on the legacy of the lion's reward and demanding greatness from yourself every day of your life.

Chapter 9 Summary Activity
My Greatness

❖ Possibility thinking is key to demanding greatness. What time will you dedicate 15 minutes a day to "soak your mind" in possibilities. Choose a time for each day.

_____

_____

_____

_____

_____

_____

❖ List your DCMVP (Most Valuable Point/Principle) from this chapter.

_____

_____

❖ Why did this DCMVP stand out to you?

_____

_____

❖ How will you use this DCMVP to change your life?

_____

_____

Conclusion

Join The Greatness Movement

The book was created not for the purpose of motivating you for a moment; it was created to help you create a monumental shift in a new direction in your life. The key to sustaining the momentum you have gained from reading this book is to connect with like-minded people. This is what will happen when you join the greatness movement by visiting www.DeAndreCarter.com for more information.

Joining the greatness movement will help you to maximize your potential, enhance your performance and explore all of your possibilities in a way that you only dreamed was possible. The synergy from other achievers will propel you forward in ways that could never happen if you were alone. Be the lion not the gazelle, and remember lions rarely hunt alone.

Once you get a true understanding of the greatness that already lives within you, then the idea of quitting will bounce off you like faster than Indian rubber ball bouncing off concrete. That negative thought would leave as quickly as it would come because of your capacity for faith --and belief would consume you to a level that would not allow doubt, fear, disbelief or the thought of quitting to reside within you. Your unstoppable nature would not only be triggered, but fully activated thus allowing you to walk in new power, new strength and new ability to change your life in ways that up to this point, you have only imagined to be possible.

My friend, this is our moment. Our time for greatness is here.

About the Author

DeAndre Carter has become recognized as a motivational force and push behind America as he challenges people to demand greatness every step in life they take forward.

Recognized as an award-winning speaker and ranked amongst the top in the world by Toastmaster's International DeAndre has been instrumental in effectively developing motivation in people that causes a response of action while naturally shifting paradigm producing a consistency and an evolutional change.

Afforded the honor and high regard to speak to audiences from America's youth and next generation leaders to college presidents and government officials to name a few. Mr. Carter's impact transcends demographics as he has extended himself for more than 15 years to over 500 audiences with life changing messages powered by practical implementation of his proven success strategies.

Mr. Carter receiving his Bachelor of Arts degree from Michigan State University in Business Marketing defines "progressive" and "innovative" in every sense by challenging society as he creates new learning platforms and tirelessly works with institutes and corporations that defy the world by provoking people to thrive. "Success is yours" is the reality that DeAndre lives by and will stop at nothing to ensure he shares this reality with the world!

To book DeAndre for your event:

Services include:

Corporate Training
and
Educational Development

www.deandrecarter.com

Please call 313-974-1269
or email: info@deandrecarter.com

Get Connected with DeAndre!

 *DeAndre Carter: Author, Speaker, Life Coach*

 *@_deandrecarter*

 *@_deandrecarter*

 *DeAndre Carter*

 The Greatness Movement

Made in the USA
San Bernardino, CA
08 July 2016